Pagan Portals
Hekate

A Devotional

Pagan Portals
Hekate

A Devotional

Vivienne Moss

MOON
BOOKS

Winchester, UK
Washington, USA

First published by Moon Books, 2015
Moon Books is an imprint of John Hunt Publishing Ltd., Laurel House, Station Approach,
Alresford, Hants, SO24 9JH, UK
office1@jhpbooks.net
www.johnhuntpublishing.com
www.moon-books.net

For distributor details and how to order please visit the 'Ordering' section on our website.

Text copyright: Vivienne Moss 2015

ISBN: 978 1 78535 161 7
Library of Congress Control Number: 2015943098

A CIP catalogue record for this book is available from the British Library.

Design: Lee Nash

Printed and bound by CPI Group (UK) Ltd, Croydon, CR0 4YY, UK

We operate a distinctive and ethical publishing philosophy in all
areas of our business, from our global network of authors to
production and worldwide distribution.

CONTENTS

For Kelvin—the love of my life, and my daughters—the light of my life. Thank you to my mom and my five sisters for your continued support, and my brother, who rests in the arms of Jesus. I love you all...
And of course, for Hekate—my Eternal Queen.
May we fly on the Wings of Enchantment...

Thank you to Elle J. Rossi of EJR Digital Art, LLC for the cover art.

Introduction – Into the Storm

Hekate: Have I not reason, beldams as you are,
Saucy and overbold? How did you dare
To trade and traffic with Macbeth
In riddles and affairs of death;
And, I, the mistress of your charms,
The close contriver of all harms,
Was never called to bear my part
Or show the glory of our art?
[From William Shakespeare's *Macbeth*]

As the storm looms on the horizon, I stand safely on my porch awaiting its arrival. There is an ominous feel to this storm and I shudder with thoughts of its destructive force. With a hushed breath I pray: *'Hekate, Lady of Storms, I beseech You, keep my home safe from harm. Guide this wayward storm away from my loved ones. Hekate, My Queen, the One I adore, as Your storm approaches I bow my head to You in reverence and trust that You will keep us safe...'*

She heard my prayers that night and has answered many more. Of the Gods I honor, it is Hekate, Queen of Witches, whom I call upon most. She is the perfect companion for my magical workings, bringing a certain flare and charm that other Gods lack. It is to Her that I turn for the protection of my home. Hekate has been worshipped as a household Goddess since antiquity. As a Cottage Witch I find working with Hekate to be very rewarding. The relationship we share has been enchanting and life-changing. It is not always easy to honor the Night Queen. She loves to throw challenges in my path, trying to trip me up in Her most bewitching way. I can feel Her laughing at me at times, shaking Her head in amusement. Often times a struggle, the challenges She sets for me have helped me to become a better magical practitioner and Witch.

A Cottage or Hedge Witch is one who lives on the borders of this world and the Otherworld. When she *rides* the hedge she often meets Spirits, both kindly and malevolent. Having Hekate as guide and companion is a wise choice to make. As the Crossroads Queen, it is She who opens the Gates and raises the Veil for us to travel to the Shadow-Lands.

It is as the Witch Mother and Lady of Crossroads that Hekate comes to me the most. She is a psychopomp, guide of souls. Hekate is Anassa Enveri, Queen of the Dead, Pale Mother, Lady of Bones, and Queen of Ghosts and Shadows. As Phileremos, Lover of Solitude, She haunts the cemeteries and deserted Crossroads, awaiting the lost souls to guide them home. I call on Hekate when working with my Ancestors, for She is the Opener of the Gate. Witches all over the world and in times past and present have called on Hekate for Necromantic workings.

This book is part devotional, part grimoire. Throughout these pages I will share my thoughts and feelings on Hekate, Queen of Witches. I know others will view Hekate differently, and that is okay, for we are all unique beings. While I have come to know Her as *Soteria*, the Savior and World Soul, it is in Her more organic form that She most often appears to me. She is Hekate Chthonia (of the Earth), Nykteria (night-wandering), Antaia (sender of nocturnal visions), and Nerteron Prytanin (Mistress of the Dead). She is my Dark Muse, bringer of inspiration. This is not an academic tome, nor one that is set in historic tradition. This is a modern view of Hekate as seen through the eyes of a solitary Hedge Witch. At the end of this book I will include a small snippet of Hekate's history along with correspondences and some of Her many epithets.

May Kalliste Hekate bless this tome...

Chapter 1

In the House of Hekate

Hekate,
You are the allure of Autumn and the madness of Winter.
You are the smell of damp earth after the passing of storms.
You are the Raven's flight and the Owl's call.
You are the soft glow of Sunset and the hoary light of the Moon.
You are the crisp breath of a Midwinter morn and the soft sigh of
  Spring's awakening.
You are the silence of Death and the enchantment of Life.
Hekate, My Queen, You are.....
[Vivienne Moss]

She Whispers in my Dreams

I first heard Her in the realm of my dreams. She was softly calling to me, beckoning me to follow. I silently shadowed Her, unsure of where we were headed. I heard birdsong in the distance and the crashing of waves. She led me to a seashore where we stopped by the entrance of a secluded cave. As I stepped into the cave a soft glow of welcoming light enveloped me. There were ancient markings on the stone walls, symbols both arcane and unfamiliar. On the floor of the cave was a small altar decorated with skulls, feathers and all manner of found baubles. Fruit, honey, and wine were laid out pleasingly, ready for this shrouded figure to consume. I looked deeply into Her primeval eyes, knowing instantly who She was. Hekate, Queen of Witches. She had claimed me as Her own. I awaken from my slumber, embracing my new self. Hekate, I whisper, I am Yours....

Many times I have traveled to Hekate's cave in Spirit Flight. She is always shrouded, Her features hidden. Only the depths of Her eyes can be seen. They go on for eternity, full of knowledge and, sometimes, sadness. She has seen all; the beginning of Earth and the slow destruction of these sacred lands. Hekate is one of the first of many Gods to inhabit this world. She is as ancient as the Starry Heavens and Her reach is far. She dwells on the borders of this world and the Shadow-Lands, Her cave safely hidden at an ancient Crossroads. It is so ancient that no memory of it survives. You can only find it during Spirit-Flight, or Hedge-Riding, much like the Witch's Mountain or Benevento.

She visits my Dream-World often, leaving hints of Her esoteric knowledge in Her wake. As I ride the currents of eternity to Her hidden cave, I feel the rush of Death pass me by. The once hidden Shadow-Lands materialize, figures emerging, both uncanny and obscene. Feeling the tug of forgetfulness, I steady my senses, bracing for the Night Queen to arrive...

And arrive She does. With each visit to Her Cave of Dreams, I grow closer to the Pale Mother—She Who is Born of Stars. For it is the stardust of dreams that gather at the tides of the seasons, bringing the Spirits of the Shadow-Lands closer to our waking world.

Hekate—I Dream with You tonight
May I elude the Spirit of Forgetfulness...

The Hearth of Remembrance

The Shadow-Lands, or Otherworlds as they are more often called, are just beyond our Earthly realm. Spirits dwell there. Some were once human, our Ancestors, but many are Spirits who have never had a human form. They have been here from the beginning, much like our Gods. Hekate, a psychopomp, is an intermediary between the living and the dead, the Spirits and mankind. She protects the home from wayward Spirits and ghosts, and guides lost souls back to their Underworld home.

Much of my work with Hekate includes my Ancestors and the Mighty Dead. A shrine dedicated to them is a main focal point in my home. It cannot be missed. When you walk into my home you can sense the uncanny, yet welcoming, feel of enchantment. Oddments of witchcraft can be found throughout my home. A feather here, a solitary stone there, an old and weathered bone tucked neatly beside a candle. The hearth houses my Ancestor shrine, candles are lit daily, fresh water offered at first light. Prayers of gratitude and reverence are whispered on hallowed breath. Trinkets of loved ones are placed lovingly on the shrine. Pictures, a pipe, a shell casing from my brother's funeral and a rose for my grandmother are but a few of the items to be found on the shrine. I can often be found reading next to the hearth, feeling comforted by the presence of my loved ones who have passed beyond the veil. This is the heart of my home. With the help of Hekate, magic is woven through the fibers of my home, enchantment and mystery live within these walls. The voices of my Ancestors are heard within my dreams.

Hekate, Lady of the Home,
As I wake in the morning I feel blessed knowing You are here.
Your essence and magic can be found in the laughter of my children
who sleep safely under Your roof. It is You who watches over us
as we sleep, sending away unruly Spirits who may cause us harm.
Hekate, Queen of the Dead,
As I lay down to sleep I thank you for bringing me closer to my
    Ancestors.
I know they are safe in the Realm of the Dead
under Your loving embrace. As the candles are spent,
Your Torches burn, guiding them home...

She Who Guards the Threshold

On the threshold of my home hangs a solitary skeleton key. This is Hekate's Key, She who Guards the Gate. With the presence of this Key only those who mean no harm may enter. It has been charged with protective charms and blessed on the altar of Hekate. Hekate is very protective of those who show Her devotion. One of Her earliest manifestations is as a Household Goddess. She was called upon to protect the home and those living within. Hekate was invoked to protect loved ones while traveling and small shrines were erected in Her honor outside the home's entrance. Every Full Moon I recharge Hekate's Key for the protection of my home as well as my loved ones. It has not failed me nor do I predict it ever will. Her Key is a very potent tool in that it helps to avert evil from entering my home. And believe me, there is evil out there. Not only in Spirit form, but also humans who can be one of the vilest of entities. I am a very protective mother of two daughters. There are those out there who can and will, if given a chance, harm them. I will do anything to stop that from happening. Knowing Hekate is there to help protect them eases my mind.

Hekate can be a fearsome Goddess. She is Brimo, The Terrifying One, causing strife to those who cross Her. She is Deinos, The Dread Goddess, Bringer of Death and Destruction. Her Hell Hounds are known to prowl the night, hunting malevolent Spirits and people. She is not one to be taken lightly. She will strike you down, leaving your rotting carcass for Her Hell Hounds to devour.

Beware Deinos — The Dread Goddess from the Worlds Below
She who is Brimo of the Crackling Flame
Hekate of the Night She is called,
She who leaves Death and Destruction in Her wake...

Hekate Brimo, I beseech thee, lay waste to those of evil nature
Bring them to their knees, destroy them all!
Hekate Deinos, I implore thee, strike fear in the hearts of evil-doers
Shred them to pieces, feed them to Your Hounds!

Beware Deinos, The Dread Goddess of the Worlds Below
She who is Brimo of the Crackling Flame
Hekate of the Night She is called,
She who leaves Death and Destruction in Her wake…

At the Altar of Hekate I Stand

Once more I stand at the entrance to Hekate's Cave. The scent of incense floats softly on the ocean breeze. The sound of the crashing surf fills my head with whispers of magic. I feel Her presence within and silently step across the threshold of Her seaside home. I find Her kneeling at Her altar, arcane chants rising from Her lips. She sips some wine, relishing its exquisite flavor. She turns to me and smiles, a hint of mischief in Her eyes. She has plans for me, I feel. Am I ready? Can I rise to the challenge? I smile back at Her, the same mischief in my eyes. I'll give it one Hell of a try…

My ever-changing altar reflects the seasons and sometimes my moods. Always present is Hekate, for it is Her altar. Here I pray and make offerings to my Queen. The lighting of Her candles and incense are a sacred event. My morning and nightly devotionals are done here, they change from day to day. I speak from the heart when addressing Her at these moments. The events of the day reflect the sacred words I express to Hekate. Some are pleads of mercy for the wrongdoing to innocents, others are prayers of gratitude for the Blessings She bestows on my family.

When weather or time do not permit me to leave offerings for Hekate at a crossroads, I make use of my outdoor altar. It sits low to the ground like most altars for Chthonic Deities. Here I carve a crossroads into the ground, placing my offering near it. Leaving it overnight, I then bury the offering the next day.

The erecting of altars is a sacred and hallowed act. It is a gift to the Gods, one that you put your heart and soul into constructing. The objects that we place on them hold special meaning to both us and our Gods. The making of charms are done there. Prayers are raised to the Starry Heavens. We cry, pouring our hearts out to the Spirits and Ancestors. Reading of runes and scrying for remnants of the past and snippets of the future are done at this sacred space. Enchanted waters and potions of healing are left on altars for the Gods to bless. All manner of witchery is done here, making this one of the most magical spaces of my home.

Hekate, My Queen
At Your altar I stand
Offering You prayers and admiration

Hekate, Queen of Witchery
These charms and enchantments are Yours to bless
May the Spirit of Magic be present in their making.

Hekate Daidalos, Cunning One
By the Hiss of Serpents You call Your Children of the Night
May we hear Your whispered enchantments.

Hekate, Dark Muse
May I continue to be inspired
By the mystery that is You...

My home has been filled with the enchantment that only Hekate can bring. She inspires me to be myself, to follow my dreams and fly on the wings of magic. I adore both the light and dark aspects of Her, for I am much the same. I can feel Her, even in this mundane world. She is just a breath away, waiting for us to awaken from the Slumber of Forgetfulness.

Hekate... Awaken my mind so I may Dream...

Chapter 2

At the Crossroads We Meet

I am standing at a Crossroads, tendrils of fog caressing me. I call for Her, Hekate, She of the Crossroads. In the distance I hear the barking of dogs. She has arrived! Shivers of excitement run through my body. I ready myself, knowing that a magnificent journey is about to begin. She gestures to the three pathways of the Crossroads, signifying that I must choose my own way—my own Destiny. On baited breath I take my first step—into the unknown...

In the Scottish Ballad *Thomas Rymer*, The Queen of Elphame explains to True Thomas the meaning of the Three Paths of Faery.

O see not ye yon narrow road,
So thick beset wi thorns and briars?
That is the path of righteousness,
Tho after it but few enquires.

And see not ye that braid braid road,
That lies across the lillie leven?
That is the path to wickedness,
Tho some call it the road to heaven.

And see not ye that bonny road,
Which winds about the fernie brae?
That is the road to fair Elfland,
Whe[re] you and I this night maun gae.
[From *English and Scottish Popular Ballads* by F.J. Child]

The many paths that we may choose to take in life are much the same as those shown to True Thomas. Though some may lead to trouble and conflict, others will lead to love and happiness. It is Hekate, Lady of the Crossroads, who guides us on our chosen paths. Yes, we choose the paths we take, but Hekate is there to shine a light on the choices we make. She is there as a gentle reminder that we are never truly alone, no matter how solitary we choose to be. Hekate, as a Goddess of Solitude, knows all too well why some may choose to walk alone in their spiritual paths. Knowing She is just a breath away eases my mind and makes me more confident in my decision to walk the solitary path of a Hedge Witch. It is but one of the paths I have chosen to take in this journey called life. As I take a step toward my destiny I know that there is power in wisdom; the wisdom to understand that, though I may not know where the path will lead, I trust in my instinct to choose the path I am fated to follow.

Hekate, Lady of the Crossroads, as You light the many paths of Destiny I stand ready to step into the unknown. I hear the Screech Owl's call, luring me in—enticing me with its peculiar cry. Suspended in the twilight air, whispers from the past try to deceive me. Ignoring the pull, I move forward—my Destiny awaits...

Through the Briar Patch

The tangled web of life's challenges can be overwhelming and solemn. There are many times that I have regretted a choice I have made only to realize that without that particular journey I would not be where I am today, nor would some of my loved ones be in my life. Like the Faery-worlds, my life has been both enchanting and peculiar. The land of Shades and Shadows has beckoned for me to walk the path of Solitude, working with the Spirits and Fae of the Dark and Shadowy realms. Though foreboding at times, those of the Shadow-Lands have proven to be beneficial in my spiritual path. It is Hekate, the Night Wandering Queen, who first showed me the Lands of Shadow. A tangled mass of briar patches guard the entrance to the Shadow-Lands, causing those who wish to enter to find their own way through. Coming out with scrapes and bruises is all part of the adventure. The roads to Faery are no different than the roads to Life. It's how we come out on the other side that matters. Resilient and full of wisdom from the trials we go through shows that we are victorious.

Hekate, my Queen, through the Briar Patch I step, ready to walk with You in the Shadow Realms. The glow of Your torches lights the way, guiding me as I fight through the tangled briars of my mind. Hekate, Light Bringer, as I clear the webs of deceit from my path I arm myself with the Power of Wisdom. The inky shadows of deception creep into the distant corners of Life, tempting me to stray from Destiny's Path. Hekate Skotia, Lady of the Gloom, it is You who pulls me from the deep, showing the way to salvation and freedom. Hekate, my Queen, with You by my side I walk the Shadow Realms with integrity and respect, coming through a stronger woman...

Paradise Lost

I stand on the horizon of Eternity waiting for The Dread Goddess to appear. Surrounded by a shroud-like mist, the feeling of vulnerability overcomes me. I take in my surroundings, noticing the distinct scent of decay. There is a death-like feel to the air, causing me to shudder with trepidation. I know She is near, I can feel Her — The Pale Mother. A sense of calm settles over me, wrapping me in its warm embrace. I hear Her soft voice, She whispers the secrets I long to know, revealing what once was...

Seduced by the promise of Paradise, we sometimes turn a blind eye to the darkness that looms over our realm. We long for the days of Eden and Avalon, when our world was pure and innocent. There are those of us who wish to re-enchant this planet we call Earth. What some of us do not realize is that it has always been enchanted, we have just lost the ability to *see* and *feel* the magic that *lives* and *breathes* alongside us. Paradise is not lost, it is being destroyed by the greed and lust of mankind. When we come to realize that Paradise is still here, still with us, we decide to reclaim this world as our own. We learn to fight for what is right, true, and just. It is when I meet Hekate at the Crossroads that I learn what is truly going on in this world. I recognize all the destruction and turmoil that consumes the Realm of the Living. There is more that goes on than we know. Hekate knows all and sees all, She opens the gate to True-Sightedness. It is at Her Crossroads that we are introduced to the hidden dangers of our world.

There are those who belong in the brighter Summer-Lands, but others, like myself, feel at home surrounded by the grim shadows of the darker realms. There is an ethereal tranquility about the Shadow-Lands that call to me. I find solace in the wildness of these lands. It is untamed and free here, full of beauty and splendor. Autumn is ever-present, the twilight air chilled to perfection. As the mists of uncanny magic swirl about me I feel empowered and free to be who I am meant to be. It is here that I reclaim my inner power and employ it in the Living World to fight against the ones who wish to destroy the worlds, both mundane and Other. The Shadow-Lands are Hekate's realm. She who is Queen of Ghosts and Shadows haunts the darker realms with the other Under-World Gods and Spirits. This is the Paradise of the Un-Seelie and Spirits of Shadow. Those who hide in the background doing all the dirty work that needs to be done in order for Hekate's light to shine through to the Land of the Living.

Hekate Noctiluca, Light of the Night, it is You who shines the Light of Truth upon the Land of the Living. Our world would be cast into eternal darkness without Your Unconquerable Flame. Anassa Hekate, Nourisher of Life, I ask You to Guide us, show us the way to

*Freedom. Hekate, the Truth is revealed through You my Queen —
may I serve You well in the Shadow-Lands...*

Down the Rabbit Hole

*I follow the serpentine path through Faery only to find myself in an
unknown land filled with mystery and mayhem. The damp air is
scented with brine and the crashing of surf can be heard nearby. I'm
sure it is near, Hekate's Cave. It can always be found by the seaside
hidden in the Mists of Time. I search for Her dwelling, not sure
where to go or in which way to turn. All around me I can hear
laughter mocking me, causing my confusion to escalate. With my
heart thrashing franticly, I turn to run — to where I know not. I
stumble and fall, landing on my knees. I look up and there She
stands. Hekate, cloaked in Her saffron robe. The howling winds
whip Her tri-colored hair about Her hooded visage. First black, then
red and finally white, Hekate's hair changes with Her tempera-
ments. I stand on unstable legs to face Her, bowing my head in
reverence. I have been fooled by these strange and uncanny lands of
Faery, pixie-led by my own fear. I look into Hekate's soulful eyes
and vow to overcome my anxieties. With newly opened eyes I find
my way to Her Cave...*

Walking the path of a Witch is full of twists and turns, learning
to navigate them is part of the adventure. I have learned the hard
way that letting my fears overwhelm me hinders my ability to
connect with the Spirits and Gods. Fear works the same way in
the mundane world. I have had to overcome many fearful situations to get where I am today. I have found taking a leap of faith
to be both exonerating and exhilarating. Like the Fool in tarot,
you sometimes have to trust in yourself and let go.

The Shadow-Lands are full of strange and sullen Spirits.
There is a seriousness to their nature, unlike the more playful
trickster types that live in the brighter realms. Sometimes called

the Seelie and Un-Seelie, these Spirits, or Fae, can help or impede us no matter which court they belong to. I have found Hekate, Queen of Shades and Shadows, to be one of the Queens of the Un-Seelie or Shadow-Folk. There will be some who disagree with me on this, but it is through my workings and conversations with Hekate that I have come to this conclusion. The Un-Seelie, or Dark Fae, are part of the Under-World Kingdom. Much like Alice discovered in Wonderland, the rabbit hole can lead to quite an adventure. Working with the Dark Spirits can be both dangerous and rewarding, but that can be said for almost anything done in life.

There is a certain rebellion that takes place when working with the Dark Spirits and Fae. We are warned against it yet we seek the freedom to explore these darker realms for ourselves. The bizarre obscurity has romanced me and I have fallen in love with the Shadow-Lands, finding my soul's path there. It is the perfect place for me, the misfit and wanderer. I have always felt drawn to the supernatural and Otherworldly powers that reside within all and feel at home with the Gods and Spirits of the Otherworlds. The call of Hekate has awakened me, leading me to a life filled with wonder and enchantment. And it all begins at Her Crossroads.

Hekate's Crossroads are not found in the waking world; they are found betwixt and between worlds. They can be found on the threshold of insanity, where the control and order of this world meet the chaos and uncertainty of the Otherworlds. It is through trance states that I have found the Crossroads. Spirit-Flight is no easy task, much care and protection must be taken. Connecting with the child within helps greatly in the preparation for the journey to the Shadow-Lands. There are Flying Ointments that a witch can use to help her in the Spirit-Flight. One must find the recipe that works best for them. Many of the herbs and oils used in Flying Ointments are of the baneful nature and one must be very careful in the preparation of these enchanted salves. To travel to Hekate's Crossroads I have used herbs sacred to Her in the Flying Ointments and Powders I make.

When I arrive at Her Crossroads I find there to be many paths that lead to numerous destinations. The type of work that needs to be done will lead me to the path or journey I choose. There are several realms that can be visited in the Otherworlds, some beautiful and lovely, others full of terror and insidious creatures. I always make sure to have a connection to the Living World in my hands so I can return when I feel threatened. Just like in 'real' life, there can be crazies out there. Learning to know who and what to trust takes time. I have what I call a Spirit Stone that I use for 'traveling'. It keeps me connected to this world and helps in the transition to the Crossroads. The making of this stone is a sacred act, the symbol I use for many Otherworldly workings.

I follow You, Hekate, into the unknown. As the Darkness surrounds me, I trust in Your presence, knowing that You, my Queen, will be there to guide and protect me on my journey. The Under-World beckons, its ghostly essence intoxicating. I am enamored by the ethereal splendor of Your court, the Un-Seelie. Hekate, my Dark Queen, know that I am Your warrior, ready to combat the forces that seek to destroy all Realms. As I stand on the threshold of Life and Death, I offer myself to You.

The Hanged Man Awaits

I find Her standing at the Crossroads examining the offerings lovingly laid, ready to feed the poor. A sacrifice is what She is waiting for. I hear Her ancient voice echo through the ages: 'Your sacrifice must be freely offered, and will take strength and determination to give. This will not be easy, sacrifices seldom are. What will you offer, dear child? What do you have to give that I do not already possess? Will it be your life, your passion—your will? Think deeply before you decide. There will be no turning back...' As the mists of uncertainty surround me, I look acutely within myself. I know what I must offer Her. Hekate awaits…

As I learn to live my life freely, I find that there are sacrifices to be made. I have had to make a sacrifice to myself in order to embrace my sovereignty. My sacrifice? To stop living to please those who I feel I need to impress. To stay true to myself, live for freedom of self with integrity and respect for others. Living for ourselves is one of the hardest things we can do. I personally was concerned with what people in my life thought about me and my spirituality. I let that fear keep me from being true to myself and the Gods and living with grace and independence. What I thought was a safe haven to hide myself was actually a prison of self-doubt that held be back from living the life I dreamed of. Not only the life of enchantment and mystery, but my mundane life as well. The fault lies with me and no other. The sacrifice of ego can be a very difficult yet rewarding journey. Escaping the prison of the past has led to the freedom of expression I have longed for. I feel resurrected from the demons of negativity that fed off my insecurity. It was Hekate's call that awakened me from my slumber of denial. I thank Her every day for opening my eyes to the enchanted world I have come to cherish.

Living with sovereignty has its risks. No longer can I hide behind my own fears, I must take a stand and walk the path of nobility. One must be strong of will and character to walk with the Gods and Spirits of Witchdom. It is not an easy path to follow and many sacrifices must be made. Not all sacrifices are the same; we must decide for ourselves what we are willing to give. The offering of self is very personal and will be different according to the circumstances. There are times that I find myself at a loss at what to offer the Gods and Spirits. Getting to personally know Them is the perfect place to start. They will guide you in the right direction and let you know if they are pleased with your offering or sacrifice.

The writing of this book is an offering to Hekate. The sacrifice is knowing that not everyone will agree with or like what I say within these pages. Some, I'm sure, will not understand the way I see and feel Hekate. I may get negative feedbacks, or worse, none at all. Maybe some will laugh or be offended with what I have written. That is a chance I am willing to take. For Hekate — for myself. Even if just one person is touched by this devotional, it will be worth it. The impact Hekate has had on my life has been a positive one and I wish to share that with the world. This devotional is a personal challenge, one that I will see to the end. It is Hekate's eternal love that pushes me forward and helps in my internal struggle to be true to myself and the Gods. Entering the Shadow-Lands as a free spirit has led to my sovereignty and the writing of this book. The independence of self has been exhilarating.

Hekate, Mistress of the Shadow-Lands, at the Crossroads of Self-Sacrifice I have found my Sovereignty hidden within the deep realms of my mind. It is You, Keeper of the Keys, who gave me the source and power to unlock the Mysteries of Self. Hekate, my Queen, as I enter the Lands of Shadow may the Spirit of Self-Doubt elude me. May I walk in Honor, free from the fear of failure. Hekate, Queen of Ghosts and Shadows, this I offer You — My undying gratitude and devotion given with Love and Freedom…

Chapter 3

At the Gates of Death

Death is but a Gateway to Life....
Trees stand almost bare, their limbs reaching for the last remnants
of the Sun's warmth as a silvery frost blankets the land. The cold
November air runs its icy fingers across my cheeks, sending shivers
of delight through my body. Everywhere I look, Death can be seen
encroaching on Autumn's bounty. I can feel the grim reality of
Death as darkness falls—the current of Life receding into the
unknown. This is Hekate's time, She who is Death's companion. I
walk with Her, into the Gates of Death, for there Life can be found
in the unexpected and unfamiliar shadows of the desolate
landscape...

Autumn leading into Winter is my favorite time of year. I feel
closest to the Gods and Nature even though the land that
surrounds me is fading into the bleak reality of Death. The
crispness of the air, the melancholy look and feel to the
environment, and the way the Sun's waning light casts shadows
upon the land inspires me. The Old Gods of Winter have
awakened from their deep slumber, revealing the magic and
mystery that lies within Death. Gossamer snowflakes dance in
the air bringing the crystalline gift of Winter's charm, and the
enchanting glimpse of the regal cardinal adds a splash of vibrant
color to the gloominess in the scenery. I can hear the voice of the
Bone Mother calling me through the blistering Arctic winds that
have roared in from the North. She who is Mother of Bone and
Stone dances with the Grim One—Death, bringing the Shadowed
World of the Dead to our doorstep. She opens the Gates of
Eternity, allowing a glimpse of the Life that dwells in the
Beyond...

Hekate, Bone Mother, as You cast Your Shadow across the lands I know that You are calling me Home, to the Shadow-Lands. I feel the pull of the beauty and awe that lie beyond Your Gates, my Queen. There I can dance with You, becoming One with You. Hekate, Mistress of the Dead, it is You who rewards us with the enchantment of Life. Through You, my Eternal Queen, I learn to Sing and Dance in the glory of Life and Death...

To Ride the Current of Death

On Owl's Wings I lift off into Mother Night, the Current of Death breathing down my neck, giving chase as I fly to Witches' Mountain — Benevento. The Old Ones are there, Gods and Witches alike, gathering to commune and celebrate with their kith and kin. Death surrounds us, enchanting us with Life and Magic. As Spirits of the Night, we feed off Death's Current, allowing it to overcome us with its raw, sensual power. We stand together, Hekate's Children, united in the faith that She is our Queen, our Witch Mother. We dance, my Sisters and Brothers of the Night, in the Ecstasy of the Death Current...for this is our Life...our Way...

The Death Current, that mysterious energy from the Shadow-Lands, draws its power from Those Who Dwell Below. It is the very essence of our Ancestors and Spirits. One day we will become part of the Death Current, joining those that have gone before, infusing the lands with life and enchantment. From Death comes Life and it is within the Current of Death that Life can be found. It is when we are met with the grim reality of Death that we cherish life and the gifts that come with it. I have lost two wonderful men to cancer and wish not for any other to endure that pain and heartache. My dad and my brother were, and still are, very dear to me. It is through their deaths that I have learned to live my life fully. To follow my dreams — to follow my bliss, as the great mythologist Joseph Campbell once said. They are forever with me and in times of need I call on them for guidance.

Hekate, Mistress of the Dead, has given me a chance to glimpse what exists beyond the Gates to the Shadow-Lands. Though it is a place where the Dead reside there is much life in these lands. The Death Current can be felt rippling through the enchanted atmosphere, filling the Shadow-Lands with a surreal life-like quality. Great feasts in vast halls are shared. Dancing, games and all manners of merriment and entertaining mayhem happen within the Lands-Eternal. It is a place where the darkly inclined can feel at home. Think film-maker Tim Burton's worlds in *The Corpse Bride* and *The Nightmare Before Christmas*, or the mysterious realm in *Alice's Adventures in Wonderland* by Lewis Carroll. There can be found both delight and terror in the Shadow-Lands. Then again, the same can be said for Tolkien's Middle-Earth.

Hekate, Nykteria, She who rules the Night, under Your guidance and protection I ride the Death Current of the Shadow-Lands. Witch Mother, Bone Mother, Night Wandering Queen — Hekate! Dance with me — fly with me — to the Lands Eternal. On the Witches' Mountain we meet, ready for the Wild Hunt — gathering all to fight in the battle of Life and Death. Nerteron Prytanin, Mistress of the Dead, in Death I find Life, in Life I rejoice in Death. Kalliste Hekate, Pale Mother, as I embrace the Current of Death I feel the enchantment of Eternal Life. Hekate, my Queen, I am Yours...

For Love of the Snow Queen

I stand on the Mountain's peak, an icy cold breath tearing through my body, wracking my soul. I call to Her, Hekate, Queen of the Shadow-Lands. In the inky blackness of the midnight air I can hear the howling of wolves, their distance unknown, any hint of direction lost in my mounting fear and desperation. In the distance I see an eerie light leading down the Mountain's side. Do I dare follow?

Where does it lead? To my doom? Or maybe my destiny... I decide to follow the wayward light, trusting in my intuition. Finally, the billowing wind subsides, allowing me to see where I am going. I notice a soft, welcoming glow growing nearer as I make my way further down the path. Enchantingly silhouetted against the snow-filled night is an ivy-covered cottage. The warmth of the hearth fire within its walls beckons me. Raising my hand to knock on the time-worn door, I shudder with uncertainty. What awaits me on the other side? Doom? Destiny? Adventure? My gut tells me all three and more are mine if I choose to cross the threshold of The Snow Queen's home...

Though not known throughout history and myth as a Snow or Winter Queen, Hekate has come to me in such a form. I feel Her in the chill of a Winter's morn and see Her in the ice crystals that form on my windows. She is the very breath of Winter, the warmth of the hearth fire, and laughter of a family gathering. There is warmth and love to be found in the Spirits of Winter. They are sometimes thought to be detached from mankind and malevolent. I think it takes a Winter-loving person to truly understand them and their Queen.

I find that the enchantment of Winter can be found in the gifts that Nature gives me. The laughter of my children playing in the snow, the snuggling in on a cold Winter's day with my lover, the birds and other wildlife that come to my yard to feast on the treats I have left for them, and best of all—dancing wildly under the snowfall. Within each unique snowflake that falls from the Heavens is a Spirit riding the Currents of Enchantment. As they touch the sacred Earth a tiny sliver of magic escapes, impregnating the land with Life Everlasting. The Snow Queen, spreading Her swan-feathered wings, enraptures the Worlds with Winter's sensuous dance. Embracing the depths of Winter, I become one with the Spirits of Frost and Ice. The erotic feel of the Arctic air upon my bare skin bring my primal self to the surface.

I dance with the Snow Queen and Her entourage, reveling in the ecstasy it brings.

Ourania Hekate, Queen of the Heavens, the snow-filled night is Yours, my Queen. As ice crystals fall from Your Celestial Realm I know that they will enchant the Lands. I dance with Your Spirits of Frost and Ice, joining my Kin in the making of Life. Oh Hekate of the Starry Heavens, Your gifts are vast, Your Wisdom great. May I feel Your Swan-feathered cloak about my shoulders, encompassing me in these darkest of nights. Hekate, Queen of Snow and Ice, You blanket the Land with the Jewels of Winter, Your crystalline magic enchanting all it touches, turning Death into Life...

In the Presence of the Bone Mother

I am once again by the seashore, the salt scented wind blowing softly, lifting my spirits on this frosty November day. Tiny shells litter the snow-white sand, adding splashes of soft color to my pallid surroundings. Standing next to me is Hekate, Mistress of Bones. At Her bare feet is a small collection of bones; human, animal, and unknown. She lowers Herself to sit, motioning for me to do the same. With the flick of Her wrist a small bonfire appears, warming us as we study the ancient offerings of the sacred dead.

'Each bone has a story to tell, a magic to give,' Hekate explains. 'The very essence of what once was still resides in them, allowing us to tap into the enchantment of the Death Current. In listening to the bones, much Wisdom can be gained. Not only Wisdom of the past or future, but Wisdom of now and the offering of Life Everlasting that it can bring.'

I listen to the wise words of the Mother of Bones, absorbing all that She has said. Picking up a precious bone, I hold it in the palm of my hand. Not only do I hear its story, I feel the pain and joy it encountered in Life and the gentle peace that Death brings to all...

As a Hedge-Witch, I have a love for bones and other baubles that Nature graces us with. The finding of discarded feathers, bewitching stones, and the death-like remnants of flora and fauna bring charm and magic to my everyday life. I use them for all manner of magical workings and the decoration of altars and tools. The bones that I find not only help me in connecting with the Death Current, they remind me that we are all destined to be in the arms of Death. Hekate, Mother of Bones, will welcome Her children into Her home when Death calls our name. She will be there, waiting with open arms and a loving heart, for She is our Mama Death, our Lady of the Holy Night. When I run my fingers across a fallen feather or touch the cool hardness of a weathered bone, I feel the connection to the Shadow Realms and Hekate. A vibrantly colored leaf in the depths of Autumn is a treasure to be found, and the first showing of a tulip's spout emerging from the late Winter's snow-covered ground, is a witness to the miraculous magic of Nature. Magic and enchantment can be found in the most innocent of moments, bringing delight to those who have the 'eyes' to see and the 'awareness' to feel. The decaying of Nature and the re-emergence of Life is a beauty to behold.

As Bone Mother, Hekate is there at the moments when the burdens we no longer wish to carry are ready to be shed and the decaying of outgrown thoughts and ideas have started to take hold. She is near, just a breath away in fact, as I call upon the Mighty Dead to bless and protect my family and loved ones. Hekate, Mistress of Bones, guards the Gateway between Life and Death, welcoming us as we join in the Dance Macabre, savoring the moments of enraptured bliss. As I walk the now bare forest, foraging for what Nature has left behind after Autumn's bounty, I cherish the life that these exquisite trinkets once carried and give thanks to the mysterious magic that they now hold within themselves.

Hekate, Lady of Bones, I give thanks for the treasures and trinkets that I have found on this bountiful Earth and honor the Life they once held. Though they have been kissed by Death, the force that dwells within enriches the lives they touch, bringing enchantment to this world and the Shadow-Lands. Hekate, Mama Death, as I touch the Bones and Stones of the Haunted Forests of Faery, may I understand the depths of their pain and dance in the footsteps of their joy. Hekate, my Eternal Queen, I join in the Dance Macabre, the Kiss of Death upon my lips as I embrace the unknown and fall into a blissful slumber only to awaken to a new world, full of Deep Beauty and Ethereal Splendor...

In the Tomb of Awakening

I find myself within an ancient churchyard, surrounded by the crumbling headstones of the forgotten Dead. A ghost-like mist rolls in, blanketing the moss covered grounds of the cemetery, giving it the feel of the Haunted Realms of the Shadow-Lands. Standing imposingly in front of me is a mausoleum, ornate iron gates protecting those who rest within. I hear whispers emerging from the depths of the vault, imploring me to open the gates and enter their Realm of Mists and Shadows. Not feeling threatened by the murmurs of the Dead, I open the heavy gates and make my way down the candlelit antechamber. A golden sarcophagus rests in the center of the baroque room, the holiness of the chamber palpable. At the foot of the sarcophagus kneels a hooded figure, head bowed in reverence. As I approach Her—for I sense that this is Hekate of the Shadow-Lands—I kneel next to the Queen of the Dead, taking Her hand in silent condolence. We weep together, for the Forgotten Ones, knowing that with their sacrifices we awaken to the glories of Life Enchanted...

It is through the trials of Death that we learn to awaken to the glories of Life. The loss of loved ones, the ordeal of a debilitating injury or disease, the letting go of harmful habits and situations, and the loss of our youthfulness can open our hearts and minds to the deepest of compassion for *all* life. Crawling out of the darkness of regret and wrapping our arms around the light of forgiveness allows us to walk with integrity and honor; the Sword of Truth cutting through all that holds us back from living our dreams. Hekate Soteria, our Savoir, stands by our side during our greatest of needs. She gives us the strength to get through the hardships and tribulations that Life throws in our paths. When I need Hekate, I pray to Her, asking for guidance and strength. I find Her to be a compassionate Goddess, lighting my way through the Darkness and leading me to my salvation—my truth. Through Her, I have learned to open my mind to the truths of Life and Death, vowing to live this life fully. Following my dreams, my bliss, my truth has opened many doors of possibility.

I have awakened to the world the Forgotten Ones left for us. The wonder and fascination they felt for this world when they were alive has been passed down to me. The waking world is as alive with magic and enchantment as the Faery Realms. The Wastelands of Today will lead to the Blessedness of Tomorrow. Hekate, Nourisher of Life, stands ready to heal the Lands.

*Hekate, Holy Creatrix, through Death I have found the Joys of Life. In Your name, I rejoice, Your Glory and Compassion filling me with Hope and Love for **All**. Hekate Soteria, Our Savior in the Saddest of Hours, I call upon Thee to shine Your Healing Light across the Lands, both Seen and Unseen. May the Wastelands of Today bring Love and Compassion to the Blessedness of Tomorrow. Hekate— Light Bringer—Heaven Shiner—Mistress of the Shadow Realms, I beseech Thee, bless the Souls of the Forgotten Ones, enriching them with Peace and Solace. Weeping tears of Remembrance and Gratitude I kneel with You, my Queen, at the Tomb of Awakening…*

Chapter 4

To Embrace the Muse

Dark mother Muse
Dread and Wild
I cannot resist you
I won't even try…
[Veronica Cummer, *Masks of the Muse*]

Dark Muse

Black as night
On Raven's wings
She conjures
Secrets in our dreams.

Arcane knowledge
And prophecy
The Dark Muse
Brings Ecstasy.

Bones and Baubles
Crystals clear
Speak of magick
Not from here.

From Shadowed Lands
She comes to test
The chosen ones
Who will not rest.

In Her Cauldron
Of Despair
She adds the treasures
That we fear.

Face your demons
That's all She asks
To follow through
Her given tasks.

Taste the Blood
Of the Grail
Those of Passion
Shall not fail.

For seven years
You belong to Her
A tythe to Hel
Are you sure?

To serve the Muse
Is Death's sweet kiss
Leading to
Inspired bliss...
[Vivienne Moss]

Seducing me with the promise of inspired bliss, the Dark Muse
consumes my every thought. Robed in the palest of green, perfumed
with the scent of anise, and the diabolically sweet taste of sugar upon
Her lips sends my senses into a whirlwind. Drowning in Her warm
embrace I succumb to the ecstasy of the moment. Hekate, Dark Muse
of the Starry Heavens, intoxicates my mind, unleashing the madness
within...

The Muse; sometimes She eludes us and other times She overwhelms us with moments of maddening inspiration. She can consume our waking moments and haunt our sleeping dreams with images and thoughts of creative visions. Hekate, the Night Wandering Queen, has, on occasion, invaded my dreams with nightmarish visions that have led to the writing of this devotional. Though often terrifying, these visions are meant to awaken the truths of the Hidden Realms of Reality. Hekate, riding Her Dark Steed of Terror, ushers in the shifting energies of creative bliss, producing flashes of divine inspiration. She is brilliant in Her manipulation of the Unseen Realms of my dreams, showing me the way through the Gates of the Shadow-Lands and the Worlds of Faery. It is in these realms that Hekate, my Dark Muse, transforms my thoughts of reality into the curious mind of a seeker. She unearths the hidden treasures of the enchanted world that surrounds me.

Hekate Antaia, Sender of Nocturnal Visions, You awaken my imprisoned mind to the realities of the Beyond, intoxicating me with the essence of creative bliss. Hekate, Queen of the Night, the Moon is Your elixir of Divine Inspiration, may I drink of its splendor and ride the Currents of Otherworldly Creativeness. Brimo Hekate, Terrifying One, You are the Nightmare that haunts my dreams, awakening the Blood of the Seeker and the Witch. Hekate, my Dark Muse, may You continue to awaken the creative possibilities of my mind…

Thirst

The thirst is overwhelming, driving me to the brink of madness. I can almost taste it, the Sacred Waters of Faery. Honeyed Wine fills the Grail of Hekate, intoxicating in its Divine infusion. The Stars of Heaven can be seen in the depths of this Holy Vessel, visions of the Unseen just beyond sight. I feel myself falling, my world spinning out of control. 'Hekate!' I cry, desperate in the wanting of Her. There is no answer, only my world falling away and the thirst—growing stronger...

I thirst for knowledge of the unknown, the occult, and divine inspiration. There are times that the hidden truths are right there, just beyond my reach—my comprehension. The wanting of it can drive me mad, like a Maenad in ritual ecstasy. I crave the allure of euphoric inspiration, the kind that drives an artist to conceive their most innovative creations. Hekate Proplaia opens the Gates of Inspiration, causing the divine current of creativeness to flow through my body, allowing me to express the way I perceive the Worlds, both Seen and Unseen. When She comes to us as the Muse, our eyes open to the possibilities of our creative selves. We may see Her in a different light, as Faery Queen, Dark Muse, or Life Itself. It is our creative minds that allow us to grasp the unknown realms of reality and generate hallowed enchantment within our lives. The thirst and hunger for the Muse strengthens me, making me strive for the rapture of creative bliss.

Hekate, Dark Muse of the Shadow-Lands, may I drink deeply from Your Grail. Hekate, Most Beloved One, I am seduced by Your Beauty and Terror, the taste of the Unknown—intoxicating. Kalliste Hekate, Mistress of the Faery Moon, within Your Otherworldly embrace I become delirious, the wanting of Your touch—unbearable. Hekate, Dark Mother Muse, from the unquiet depths of my mind I awake, opening myself to the divine possibilities of creation, drowning in the currents of inspiration...

Born of the Stars

I am surround by the Fire of Stars, their light warming me in the cold Winter night. Mother Nyx stretches Her ebony wings across the skies, sheltering all the Worlds, Seen and Unseen. The Star

Mother, Asteria, comforts Her children, the Stars, as they ready to fall from the Heavens. Hekate, Daughter of the Starry Heavens, guides Her brothers and sisters to the Earthly Realms below. Like ash from a fire, they blanket the Worlds; Star-Dust—the beginnings of Life...

We are all born of the Stars, equal in the Celestial Dust that is within us. It is what binds us, what connects us with all life. Through the flow of Star-Dust we interact with the Spirits of the World, sharing in the divine flow of The Great Song of Inspiration. Hekate, Opener of the Gates, allows the Star-Dust to flow freely between the Realms. When I drink of Her cup, Her Sacred Grail, I allow the divine elixir of inspiration to enter my Spirit. Just before drowning in the rich muse-like mixture, I pull myself from the depths of the Grail, my creative expression flowing out into the Worlds.

Star-Dust; it is the fire that burns within, the spark that ignites the passion I feel for the world around me. It is life—desire—bliss, it is what enchants all the Realms. Star-Dust—Star-Fire, it flows within all, it is our blood, our soul, our breath. Hekate, Daughter of the Starry Heavens, is of the Stars. She *is* the Star of Life. She is the Holy Light that shines upon the Worlds, a beacon in these dark times. Her light—*Her* essence is the inspiration that flows out from the Starry Heavens enriching our lives with creative passion. Hekate, Fair One of the Night, shines forever in our lives, enlightening our minds and hearts with the Fire of Creation.

Kalliste Hekate, Fairest Queen of the Night, Your Star-Fire blankets the lands, bringing peace and tranquility to the Worlds. Hekate, Daughter of the Starry Heavens, as we dance under Your Ethereal Light, may we drink deeply from the Well of Inspiration, becoming one with our creative selves. Hekate, my Queen, the lunacy within shatters, Star-Dust fills the void of nothingness as the Faery Moon blinds the unwise...

Touched by Madness

Bathed in moonlight, I step out of my clothes and let the cool air kiss my skin. As I sway to the melody of the night, my mind and body break free from the shackles of the mundane world. The primal need for erotic liberation takes over. In frenzied delight my lone dance quickens until, finally, I collapse to the dew-kissed ground. The beautiful madness of the ritual is witnessed by the Star-filled night; The Pale Mother sighs, pleased with my offering of ecstatic dance...

The Moon, Mother of Lunacy, entices us to break free of the bonds that deny us our creative and carnal expression. It births divine madness, kissing our minds and hearts with poisoned delight. When I gaze at the Moon in all Her splendor, I feel the need to dance under Her spell-like light. The primal urge to connect with my animal-self is impossible to resist. I can feel the Spirits of the Shadow-Lands join me in this sacred dance, the raw power of the moment binds us. We become one under the Light of the Pale Mother, our minds and bodies infused with ecstasy. I am my true self when I let down my guard and allow my primal nature to take over, even if just for a moment of ritual madness.

Hekate Noctiluca is the Light of the Night, the Night Shiner. She is one of the many Moon Goddesses, shining Her ethereal light down from the Heavens. She casts Her spell on many, causing lunacy and divine madness. To be touched by Her — kissed by Her, is an experience to be treasured. When the Dark Muse enters your life, be ready for the creative impact She will have on you. She can cause an obsession that is quite maddening, the allure of Her touch — addictive. When She disappears from our sight we cry out in despair, wanting Her to return to us in all Her glory. And when She does, when She re-enters our lives, we are wise to pay Her honor and thank Her for the inspiration She bestows upon us. For if we don't, we will soon regret our foolhardy ways.

Hekate Noctiluca, Light of the Night, within Your diabolically sweet embrace I awaken to my creative self. Hekate, Pale Mother, Your touch brings welcomed Madness, I am consumed by its power. Hekate, my Queen, as You cast Your spell of Lunacy upon me, I succumb to the monster within, unleashing the primal spirit hidden deep within my psyche. Hekate, my Dark Muse, I dance to Your Great Song, lost in the seductive melody of enchanted bliss and the Maddening Light of the Faery Moon...

Chapter 5

Our Lady of the Witches' Craft

The scent of incense fills the air as arcane words are spoken on whispered breath. The circle is cast, the ring of Fae Fire glows with a ghost-like luminescence. Feeling the sacredness of the moment, I bow my head to the Spirits who have joined me in this rite. Hekate's presence can be felt, Her powerful essence fills the ritual space with a preternatural awe. I can feel the magic of the Ancients enter my body, infusing me with enchanted bliss. Power pulses through my senses, I am at one with the Spirits of Witchcraft. Hekate, the Witchmother, embraces me, welcoming me into Her circle—Her home...

The life of a Witch is one filled with the awe of the worlds—Seen and Unseen; it is for the curious of mind, the seeker of arcane knowledge, and for those who live on the boundaries of the Shadow-Lands. Hekate, Queen of Witches, has sounded the call for Her children to gather and drink of the magic and awe of the Earth and Her sister worlds, the Lands of Faery and Spirit. I have embraced the mystic within, coming home to my Mother, Hekate. She is Witchmother, Queen of the Hallowed Mysteries, and Guardian of Occult Knowledge.

I have become a Seeker, searching for the Truth of the Worlds. The mysteries that sleep within the Land of Enchantment entice me to walk the path of a Witch. I am forever on this journey, the adventure of the hunt—inspiring. As the Witches' Goddess, Hekate lights the way on the Road of Enchantment and Sorcery. She opens the Gate of Mysteries, revealing the hidden truth of the Ancients. The Witchmother, always existent within Nature, is the terrible beauty of a storm and the ethereal mist of the dawning fog; She is the sacred land we walk upon and the sensual touch of our lover. Hekate, Our Lady of the Witches' Craft, is the ever-lasting Space of Time and the ever-present Winds of Destiny.

Anassa Hekate, Queen of Witches, You enchant the Worlds with Your Song of Eternity, Your ethereal voice charming the Hearts of All. Witch Mother, Queen of Mysteries, I walk the Path of Enlightenment in search of the Hidden Treasures of the Mystic, the Hunt enticing in its allure of Truth. Hekate, My Eternal Queen, as I travel along the Path of Witchery, may I be enriched with the Knowledge of the Ancients and the Sensual Beauty of the Worlds....

Into the Woods

Through the tangle of the Forest's deep-rooted trees, I find my way to the Witches' Cottage. Hidden from view by a canopy of deep shades of green, the enchanted haven beckons for me to enter. As I cross the threshold, the time-worn floorboards creak under my easy footsteps.

Hung from the rafters are fragrant bunches of dried flowers and herbs; to my left is the hearth fire, a cauldron of rosemary-infused stew simmers in the warmth of the flames. There is a table nearby, a veiled woman sits quietly, She watches me under a steely gaze. The clove-scented woman opens Her hands to me, a gesture of welcome to join Her at the old wooden table. There are a variety of bones and baubles spread out on the tabletop. The Witchmother, for I sense that it is She under the gossamer veil, gathers them into Her hands. Knowing that She is wanting to cast the lots for me, I concentrate on what I wish to be revealed. The Witchmother Hekate, with a quick flick of Her delicate hands, casts the bones and baubles onto the cloth that awaits these sacred treasures. Looking deep into my eyes—my soul, Hekate reveals what is Fated to be...

Deep within the Enchanted Forest of our lives are cloaked the mysteries that must be revealed. Hekate, Dame Fate, holds the

Key to these most treasured secrets, unlocking them the moment She deems us worthy of knowing this arcane knowledge. She weaves a tapestry of symbols, divining the hidden truths of our desires and destinies. Hekate conceals the hidden gateway between the Worlds, lifting the Veil of Forgetfulness so we may redeem what has been lost to us, our connectedness to the Realms—Seen and Unseen. Through ritual and magic I have found my way through the tangled web of deceit that has been spoon-fed to us in this ordinary world we call home. Learning to free our minds to the Mysteries of the Beyond will lead to an uncertain voyage that only a true seeker will appreciate. Finding the enchanted cottage hidden deep within the Forbidden Forest of my unlocked awareness sets me free from the constraints of humanity. I find myself able to roam the Realms of Mystery and Shadow, discovering the hidden truths of my life and reality.

Hekate, Fated One, You reveal the Secrets of the Beyond, allowing me to find the Truth of my Destiny. Veiled One of the Hallowed Night, I bow to You my Queen, Keeper of Mysteries, may I walk the Path of Truth with honor. Hekate, Shadowed One, You light the way through the Sacred Forest of the Hidden Realms, revealing the twisted trails of enchantment—may I find my way to the Holy Temple, awakening to the Deep Below...

Weaving the Great Below

I awake to find myself within the Cave of Voices, ancient whispers of enchantment echo from the deep. Tendrils of moss-covered roots pull at me, hindering my ability to find the source of the Voices that call to me. Breaking free from the unruly tangle of vines, I make my way down the cave's tunnel. Softly lit by the light of Silent Stars, I can make out ancient symbols carved into the stone walls, their meanings lost through the mists of time. I feel the pull of remembrance as I draw closer to the Voices. I step into an antechamber, temple-like in its exquisiteness. Sitting at an ornate spinning wheel, garbed in the most sensual of fabrics, I find Hekate, Queen of the Great Below. The Voices of Many become the hauntingly beautiful Voice of Hekate. The Threads of Life and Death are at Her hands; the Thread of Enchantment visible beneath the Shadowed Light of Silent Stars. Softly She chants, charms of the arcane charge the air, the magic of the moment — palpable. The Mother of Fate releases the Dark Hallows into the Realms, the Creative force of Nature runs Deep within all…

Within every being dwell the Threads of Fate, the threads that connect us all with Nature and the Lands of Faery. The Voice of Hekate can be heard upon the Winds of Change, charging us with a call to action, a call to embrace the Sacredness of the Land, Seen and Unseen. Deep within the Earth hide the tides of rebirth, a vision of innocence woven within the Tapestry of Life. Hekate sits upon Her Dark Throne of Life and Death, weaving the Dream of Enchantment through the fabric of the Worlds. The Great Below is where all life begins, it is where the Dreamer awakens to the reality of Nature. Hekate cuts the Threads of Illusion, allowing us to see what lies beyond the Gates of the Shadow-Lands and Faery.

Hekate, Queen of Fate, holds the Dark Mirror of Time, its reflection divining the tides of the future — that which must become, revealing our distant past — that which has been, and reminding us of the here and now — that which must be. As I gaze into the dark glass of Hekate's Mirror I can feel the World's emerging through the boundaries of existence. What is revealed is at times frightening, but always alluring, leading to the abandoned, wild places of my mind. To contemplate the journeys I have been on and those that are sure to come brings me closer to that which I seek — the Mysteries of Nature and Faery, indefinable in their existence.

Anassa Hekate, Queen of the Great Below, as You Weave the Threads of Life and Death upward into the Sleeping Land, the Thread of Enchantment consumes the Waking World, connecting All that is. Dark Mother of Fate, through You, my Queen, I embrace my Fated Destiny, the journey of my Life—fortunate beyond belief. Kalliste Hekate, Fair Seer of the Shadow-Lands, Your Dark Mirror of Time and Fate reveals what is Hidden from view, allowing me to find the Treasures of Eternity...

Over the Moon-Lit Hedge

She appears, the Cunning One, just beyond the Moon-Lit Hedge, awaiting those who search for the Wild Beyond. Spirit Flight grips me, on Raven's wings I take to the Night. The Stars beneath the Land guide me to the Realms of Enchantment. The Angel of Awakening emerges, consuming all within Her reach. The Blood of Witch and Faery courses through my veins, arousing the Sleeping Power of Nature within. Hekate, Witch Mother of the Shadow-Lands, beckons for me—luring me in with Her Beautiful Darkness. I am drunk from the Power that is Her—consumed by divine madness, I embrace All that is and All that will be, becoming one with the Deep Below. I walk among the Holy, those who have gone before—the Mighty Dead of the Witches' Path. Through Blood and Star-Light I walk, searching for Truth. The Deep Well of Being quenches my thirst for knowledge, drowning the grave memories of the past. I hear Her melodious laugh, Hekate knows I have found the Mystic's Way—the Path of Enlightened Reality...

As I embrace the Blood of Enchantment that runs through my whole core, I become one with Hekate and the Spirits of the Shadow-Lands. Beneath the starlit sky I fly over the Hedge of Enchantment, finding myself deep within the Realm of the Unseen. I catch a glimpse of creatures; they flit like phantoms through the Deep Green Grove of Faery. A mix of human-like, animal, and insect forms, these organisms of Faery are like nothing I have ever seen before. They are full of Beautiful Terror and their uncanny existence rips through my once-sane mind. These are the monsters we were warned about as children, the monsters that lurked in our closets and under our beds.

But they are not monsters to be feared; these misunderstood Spirits of Faery and the Shadow-Lands are the very beings who watch over us as we grow in this mundane world of the Living. They are our Spirit-Helpers, our Familiars — our 'Guardian Angels' so to speak. We were frightened as children because our sensible minds could not comprehend what we were seeing. We were trained and taught to fear those of the Unseen Realms. These Spirits of Faery live beneath the limitless starlit sky, they are our cousins and co-walkers within the worlds Seen and Unseen. They can be understood as our Other-Selves, part of our very being. As our perceived world shifts, the Otherness of the Fae World enhances our view of connectedness. We realize that we are part of the Hidden Realms, part of Nature and Her attendant Spirits. The Earth is peppered with the Otherness of the Shadow-Lands, the very Breath of Life exists within All.

The Song of Enchantment can be heard in the graceful birdsong as it ripples throughout the Lands. Hekate, the Fair Queen of Elphame, is the sensuous touch of Nature. She is Queen of Sorcery, the Witches' Goddess, and the Dark Queen of the Shadow-Lands. She is uncanny in Her nature, the Spirits of the Shadow-Lands flock to Her for She is their Queen — their Mother. It is Hekate who sends to us our Familiars, our Daemons who are part of our lives and who become one with us in Death…

Hekate, Fair Queen of Elphame, I give thanks to You, my Queen, for my Other-Self — my Co-Walker in the Lands Eternal. Brimo Hekate, Terrifying One, Your Dark Beauty is awesome to behold, I am spell-bound by Your uncanny Nature. Dread Queen of the Worlds Below, Your limitless magic vibrates throughout the Lands, the essence of

Life and Death are within Your grasp. Hekate, Cunning One, the Wild Beyond of Delight is hidden Deep within the Dark Green Grove, may I rejoice in the finding of the enchanted worlds of Faery...

Chapter 6

The Breath of Life

The Spring-tide breeze rustles the newly born leaves, the scent of lilac fills the air. The warmth of the Sun is welcome after the endless Winter chill. The sounds of Nature surround me, the World is animated with the stirrings of Life. She breathes the World into reality, the Realm of Faery touches the Waking World—a sigh of Deep relief can be felt throughout the Lands—Seen and Unseen. Hekate, the Eternal Flame of Existence, awakens from Her slumber—the Worlds are alive with Magic as the Song of Faery rises from the depths of the Lands Below...

She is the eternal flame that burns within All, the Fire of Illumination, and the hidden spark of Divine Inspiration. Hekate, the Breath of Life, can be felt in the awakening of Spring, the exuberance of Summer, the ripeness of Autumn, and the deep slumber of Winter. She is everywhere and nowhere all at once, She is the All, the Void—the Vault of Heaven. Hekate Soteria is the Soul of the World, the Holy Creatrix of the Cosmos, and the Re-birther of Souls. She is Lady Wisdom, full of grace and compassion. Her Sacred Torch lights the way to salvation as She guards the Gates of Life and Death.

Hekate can be found in the smallest of pebbles and in the deep abyss of the sea. She is of the Heavens, the Earth and the Holy Waters. Three-Formed, She rules the Realms, universal in Her holiness. I have come to know Hekate as a Mother, a Sister, and a Companion on the path of the Witches' Craft. She can be found at the Crossroads of Change, challenging us to be true to ourselves and to uphold justice. She is the force of Nature, that which breathes Life into All.

Hekate Soteria, Soul of my Soul, I honor You always, my Queen. Lady of the Night, it is to You I turn for protection and strength, the weight of the Worlds are Yours to endure, may I ease the burden upon Your shoulders. Hekate, Light of my Life, You fill me with Your Grace and Compassion so I may share Your glory with All. Anassa Hekate, I adore You my Queen, to be in Your presence is a blessing I will cherish for an Eternity...

Beautiful Darkness

Her beauty is intoxicating, it radiates from her soul enveloping All who are in Her presence. She is ever young, a nymph in all Her splendor. Hekate, the Dark Maiden of the Shadow-Lands, graces the Worlds with Her Beautiful Darkness. As I gaze into the endless depths of Her eyes, I feel drawn to the seductiveness of Her, wanting to be one with Her. I am in love with this Dark Queen of the Underworld, She is All that is Beautiful and Enchanting — She is Eternal Love and Ecstasy...

Hekate, the Eternal Maiden of the Hidden Realms, envelopes the Worlds in ethereal beauty. She shows Her maiden side to me, for that is how She first appeared to the Ancients. She is Beauty, She is Rapture — She is Seduction. Yes, Our Dark Lady Hekate has a more primal, animalistic side. This is the Hekate who appears when danger is on the horizon, when our enemies are plotting against us. But the Hekate of Nature, of the Heavens, and of the Holy Waters is a Beauty to behold. She is the Wonder of the Enchanted Gardens, the Serpent of Wisdom is Hers, and the Worlds are Hers to rule with love and justice. She is Kalliste Anassa, the Fair Queen of the Shadow-Lands and Faery.

In Her ethereal Beauty can be found the richness of Nature, the abundant wealth of enchanted bliss hidden deep within emerges as we come to know Her as our Queen and Mother. Hekate, the Eternal Nymph, enraptures the Worlds with the magic of love and bliss. Her Waters of Creation rain down from the Heavens, bringing renewed Life to the lands, Seen and Unseen. She is Life, Love and the Compassionate One, She is Beauty and Serenity, the Wisdom of the Worlds are hidden within Her. Hekate heals the Great Sorrows that wreak havoc in our lives and the Worlds Beyond.

The velvet-soft wings of a butterfly hold the beauty of the worlds within their colorful patterns, the flight a bird carries a wish to the Fair Queen of Elphame, and the gentle winds kiss my sun-warmed cheeks. These are the gifts of Nature as the green fire at the Heart of Faery envelopes me with enchantment and splendor.

Kalliste Anassa, Fair Queen of Elphame, the Splendor of the Worlds live within You. Hekate, Beautiful Darkness of the Realms Below, You breathe Life into Death and Death into Life, enchanting us with Otherworldly Reality. Hekate, Queen of Sorrows, You hold within You the Burdens of the Worlds, healing those who whisper Your sacred name upon the Winds of Eternity. Hekate, Hekate, Hekate...

Mother of Dragons

On the Wings of Eternity I fly, enraptured by the Eternal Bliss of Her Sacred Flames. Hekate, Mother of Dragons, devours me—I re-emerge newly born as Her child. I can see the Worlds with fresh eyes now; all about me are wonders to behold, I am surround by Her Blessedness. I have awakened the dormant power of the Witch-Blood hidden within, the Throne of Sovereignty is mine, I am Queen unto myself...

She is the Serpent in the Garden, the Great Dragon of Sovereignty, and the regenerative force of Life. Hekate, Re-birther of Souls, is the Void of the Abyss, that which holds all potential. She is the wise voice of reason, whispering in our ears the secrets of living with grace and honor. Hekate, the Knowing One, is the Divine Oracle. She Dreams the future into existence and reveals the treasures of the past. She is the burst of energy as it rises through our spines, igniting our passion for Life and Love. Hekate is temptation, Her exotic beauty luring us into Her Mysteries. She is the Serpent's Kiss, regenerating our urge to delve deeper within ourselves, finding our way to Sovereignty.

Hekate, the Eternal Flame of the Worlds, ignites the life force within All. She is the Sleeping Dragon beneath the Sacred Earth, awakening to the call of Her Children, the men and women who are Her eternal Priests and Priestesses. I have answered the call to be an Oracle and Witch of Our Lady of Dragons. I am a Priestess of Hekate, I am devoted to Her in this Path of Mysticism. She calls to me from the depths of Hades and the heights of the Starry Heavens. The Mysteries of Hekate are ours to discover, their secrets—ours to decipher.

It is within the strength of the Lady of Dragons that we gather to fight for our Sovereignty; our Freedom to be, to live, to love… Under the protective wings of Hekate, the Dragon Queen, we learn to take flight into the unknown, discovering our true potential. We stand strong in the face of adversity, conquering ours fears and foes. We rise from the ashes of our failures, stronger than ever before and ready for battle.

Hekate, Mother of Dragons, by the Serpent's Kiss I have come to know You, my Queen; You are the Breath of Life, the Fire of Passion and the Holy Waters of Creation. Hekate Daeira, Knowing One, through You I grow Wise, the Secrets revealed through rapturous trance. Hekate, Re-birther of Souls, I have risen from the ashes of my past, embracing the Priestess within, becoming Your vessel, Your Child of the Mysteries—Your Daughter of Dragons…

In the Garden of Elysium

I have tasted of the Fruit of the Dead, my lips still sticky from the ripe, red juice. I walk among the Sacred as torches light the way to the Temple of Hekate. There is an ethereal beauty all around me, trees heavy with fruit scent the air with honeyed sweetness. I find myself gently swaying to the sound of birdsong, their melodious music charming all who hear their song. I am at peace here, at home with my fellow Mystics. The sacredness of Elysium is palpable, the Garden of Enchantment a sight to behold. Hekate, in all Her Holiness, awaits us, calling us to Her Sacred Temple—our true home and destiny...

When we open our eyes to the Sacredness that surrounds us we become enriched with a Deep love for Earth. We come to realize that this world can become like Elysium, the Garden of the Hesperides, Avalon, the Blessed Isle, and Eden. We can learn to live in harmony, showing love and compassion for those who share this plane of existence. At times I find it difficult to see the Sacredness of this world. War, murder, rape and greed can be found everywhere. I dream of a time when we, as humans, can find the Holiness that lives within All. A time when we become wise and compassionate, full of the beautiful grace we are capable of.

The Worlds, Seen and Unseen, are part of a whole. They are interconnected, as are those who dwell within their Realms. We are all one in the Sacred Gardens of Eternity. Hekate Soteria, The Holy Queen of All, encompasses the Worlds, guiding all to the Isle of the Blessed. She is the Mystery we seek within, the Enchanted Gardens of our Dreams, and the Passion that fills our waking desires. Anassa Hekate reigns supreme, guarding and guiding Her chosen ones, charging them with the will and desire to re-enchant the Waking World.

Bird-song fills my heart with hope and the tranquil essence of an Eden-like world. The glory of Nature surrounds me as I soak in the warmth of the noon-day Sun. The winds whisper stories of worlds long forgotten. The sacred myths of yesterday enrich the kingdom of today. Echoes of the past reach into the future. Magic and enchantment can be felt in every breath I take.

I can sense the Old Ones, their energy is ancient and filled with the Wisdom of the ages. A rock, pebble or stone holds the memories of our Ancestors and the Spirits of the Unseen Realms. A single leaf gently falling from a tree is a wish—a message from the Gods, Spirits and Faery.

This is the world I see, the world I know, the world I love. Hekate, Mother of All, encompasses this World and those Beyond, enriching my life with the Deep Beauty of the Shadow-Lands and the Erotic Love of Faery...

Anassa Hekate, as I walk through the Garden of Elysium I find myself wanting more. More Beauty and Deep Peace in the Waking World, more Compassion, Love and Enchantment. Hekate, Mother of Eternity, I beseech You, shine Your Holy Light on the Worlds, kindling the Spirit of Blissful Life. Hekate Soteria, Holy One, it is You who brings Death only to give Life Eternal. Hekate of the Blessed Isle, I have crossed the Sea of Death to find the Mystery that is You—Life Enchanted...

Of Sun and Moon

I am content beneath the noon-day Sun, soaking in Her warmth like a slumbering cat. Swathed in the liquid gold of the Day-Star, I am rich in health and vitality. There is peace here, beneath this vibrant light, the pleasures of the Worlds are mine. I stretch, relishing the scene of vibrant colors painted upon the sky. The languid air stirs memories of times gone by. I close my eyes—just a small nap is all I need...time for treasured Dream-land...

I awake to find myself beneath the Moonlit sky. She shines in all

Her glory, Selene of the Silvery One. This is the Land of Illusion, the Land of Dreams and Nightmares. I find myself ravenous here, wanting more of the Mysteries of Hekate. Reflections and precarious visions shine upon the crystal clear waters, prophecy is mine to reveal. I am mad here, delirious with primal need. I throw back my head and howl into the Night; I am free and wild, one with Nature and Passion. Shedding my skin I run with the Wolves of the Night. I am lost in ecstasy…

I am light and dark, mad and sane. I embrace all that I am and all that I can be. I step off the well-worn path to follow the twisted path of my dreams. Hekate, Lady of the Heart's Desire, leads the way; She is there to guide me along my chosen path of the Shadow-Lands and Faery. I find comfort under the Golden Light of Her Sun and a certain serenity under the Silvery Light of Her Moon. I dance amongst Her Stars, the Deepening Twilight of the Shadow-Lands fill my soul with longing, the longing of the wildness of my child-self—my Fae-self. To be free to run through the Worlds, dancing under the Moon, soaking in the Sun, swimming through the sacred Waters and playing with the Wild Ones of the Unseen Realms.

I am of Moon and Sun, Star-light and Rain, Earth and Faery. I am Nature, pure and untamed, able to be at One with All. I am at one with Hekate, for She resides within my Soul—She resides within All. Hekate, Queen of the Lands Eternal, is magic and enchantment, She fills the Worlds with the abundant peace of tranquility. She is Light and Dark, Night and Day, Life and Death—She is the All-encompassing Passion that drives us to thrive for the re-enchantment of our lives. Hekate, wild and free, is the driving force of Nature. She cannot be tamed, She cannot be denied. She is Hekate, Queen of the Shadow-Lands—Queen of All….

Hekate, my Queen, I honor You above all, You who are of the Earth and Heavens, the Sun and the Moon, and the Deep Eternal Sea.

Kalliste Hekate, Fair Queen of the Shadow-Lands, I walk the twisted path of Shadow, I am Your Priestess — Your Witch. Night Wandering Queen, I join You under the Stars and the Deep Twilight of Dreams, wild and free we run, embracing the Fae within. Hekate, Dark Mother, as I wander the Lands Eternal in search of the Mysteries, I find my Home, my Soul — I find You...

So ends my devotional to Hekate, Queen of the Shadow-Lands. In the final chapters I will share a brief history of this Great Goddess along with Her many epithets and correspondences. I will reveal some recipes for enchanted waters, magical dirt, and herbal blends along with some musings on the enchanted life of a Witch and Priestess of Hekate.

May Kalliste Hekate continue to bless my life with Her divine presence and protection...

Chapter 7

Hekate—She Who Is All

Though we may never know the true origins of the Witch Goddess Hekate, we can be sure that She is always near. She is ever ancient and ever young, a Goddess of the Ages. Hekate has been linked with many cultures and countless Goddesses. She makes Her first written appearance in Hesoid's *Theogony* and graces the pages of William Shakespeare's glorious works. Hekate is ever-changing, morphing into a beautiful nymph and a monstrous hag. She appears to us in ways that are incomprehensible to others, but make perfect sense to Her chosen ones. Hekate may be a Dark Goddess to some and a Goddess of Light to others. To me She is both Light and Dark; She holds within Her the potential of All.

The brief information flowing through the following pages are both historical and modern. Some will be from my personal gnosis and others will be from written materials of the past and present. I urge others to come to know Hekate through meditation, trance work, the study of ancient and modern texts, and devotion. She will reveal Herself to those who pay Her honor and reverence and to those who come to Her with compassion and respect. The following information can be used to construct prayers, invocations, evocations, spells, charms, incense, offerings, and the summoning of Spirits connected to the Witch Mother.

Origins

Her true origins are unknown. She has been said to originate in Thrace then move on to Asia Minor. Hekate is also believed to be Karian and has been linked to the Minoans through their Snake Goddess. She had temples in Lagina and Caria and was a guardian of Byzantium (Istanbul). My belief is that She is older than Time, She is one of the Old Ones that originated with the Waking of the Worlds. For a more concise history of Hekate please read *Hekate: Liminal Rites* and *Hekate: Keys to the Crossroads* by Sorita D'Este and David Rankine.

Parentage

There are a few Gods who have been linked with the parentage of Hekate. Like Isis, Hekate is seen to be both the Mother of All and having parents. This is a common theme throughout mythological history.

Asteria (Starry One) and Perses (Destroyer) — from Hesoid's
Theogony
Demeter — from the Orphic Hymns
Nyx (Night) — from the poet Bachylides
Asteria and Zeus — from Mousaios
Aristaios — from Pherecydes

Children

At times Hekate is said to be childless and at others She is also said to be a mother. There is no wrong way to interpret this for She is the Mother of Witches and we are Her Children of the Night.

Scylla
Circe
Medea
Chalciope
Aegialeus

Mystery Cults

Eleusinian Mysteries at the Temple of Eleusis
Orphic Mysteries

Visage

Hekate can be seen in singular and triple formed depending on the nature of Her contact. In Her most ancient appearance She is a beautiful nymph; not until recent times has She been portrayed as a crone/hag. Hekate is most commonly flanked by Her Hounds, though She can be seen with lions as well. When in triple form She can have the heads of animals and is shown holding one of Her many sacred objects.

Hekate often appears to me saffron-cloaked (Krokopelos), Her countenance veiled by a hood. When in triple form She appears as three young women; the first with red hair, the second with black hair, and the third with white hair. The emblems She carries vary with the message She is conveying.

When seen with the heads of animals, they are most often those of:

Cow/Bull
Dog
Dragon
Goat
Horse
Serpent

Names and Epithets

Like Her origins, the meaning behind Her name remains a mystery. Spelled Hekate (Greek) or Hecate (Roman), Her name is most often translated as meaning *Influence From Afar, Worker From Afar,* or *The Distant One.* It has also been interpreted as *The Most Lovely One* and *Most Glorious.* Like the Great Goddess Isis, Hekate has many names and epithets. I continue to discover more as I honor this most gracious Goddess.

For a list of more epithets of Hekate please visit *Singing For Her* by Neheti on Tumblr: http://nehetisingsforhekate.tumblr.com

Anassa (Queen)
Arkui (Spinner of Webs/Entrapper)
At the Gate (Empylios)
Averter of Evil (Alexeatis)
Beautiful Darkness
Bone Mother
Born of the Stars
Brimo (Angry One, the Terrifying One, of Crackling Flame)
Celestial/Heavenly (Ourania)
Daidalos (Cunning)
Daemoness of Sorcery
Dame Fate
Dark Maiden
Dark Mother
Dark Muse
Dark Queen
Daughter of the Starry Heavens
Drakaina (Dragoness)
Fair Queen (Kalliste Anassa)
From Afar
Funeral Queen
Goddess of Fate
Goddess of the Crossroads
Goddess of the Night
Hekate Chthonia (of the Earth)
Hekate Soteria (Savior) (World Soul)
Holy Creatrix
Huntress (Agrotera)
Infernal One
Kalliste (Fairest)
Keeper of the Key (Kleidoukhos)
Keeper of the Keys of the Cosmos (Pantos Kosmou Kleidokhos)
Lady of Bones
Lady of Storms

Lady Wisdom
Light Bringer
Light of the Night/Night Shiner (Noctiluca)
Lover of Solitude (Phileremos)
Lyco (She-Wolf)
Mistress of Corpses
Mistress of Magic
Mistress of the Dead (Nerteron Prytanin)
Mistress of the Sea
Mistress/Lady (Desponia)
Moon Goddess
Mother of Angels
Mother of Dragons
Mother of Phantoms
Nature (Physis)
Night Wandering (Nyktipotos)
Night Wandering Queen
Nourisher of Life (Zootrophos)
Nurse of Children/Protectress of Mankind (Kurotrophos)
Of the Dark/Gloom (Skotia)
Of the Path (Endodia)
Of the Sea (Einalian)
Of the Three Roads (Trioditis)
Of the Three Ways (Trivia)
Of the Underworld (Aidonaea)
One That Transforms (Ameibousa)
Pale Mother
Protectress of Flocks, Sailors, and Witches
Psychopomp (Guide of Souls)
Queen of Elphame
Queen of Faery
Queen of Ghosts and Shadows
Queen of Sorrows
Queen of the Dead (Anassa Enveri)

Queen of the Shadow-Lands
Queen of Witches
Rebirther of Souls
Ruling over All (Pasimedousa)
Saffron-Cloaked (Krokopeplos)
Savage Huntress/Temptress
Savior (Soteria)
Sender of Dreams
Sender of Ghosts
Sender of Nocturnal Visions (Antaia)
Serpent Girded
Serpent/Dragon Queen
She of the Night (Nykteria)
Tender Hearted
Tender/Delicate (Atalos)
The Distant One
The Dread Goddess/Queen (The Deinos)
The Knowing One (Daeira)
The Light Bringer (Hekate Phosphoros)
The One Before the Gates (Propylia)
The Veiled/Concealed/Hidden One
Three Formed (Trimorphos)
Three Headed (Trikepholos)
Torch Bearer (Dadophoros)
Torch Bearing Holy Daughter of the Night
Unconquerable/Untamable Goddess (Adamantaea)
Universal Queen (Pasikratea)
Virgin (Parthenos)
Wanderer of Mountains (Ouresiphoites)
Witch Mother

Attendant Beings

These are some of the Gods, Goddesses, and Spirits who are conflated with or connected to Hekate. They can be called upon in spell-work and prayers in addition to Queen Hekate. Some are benevolent and others malevolent.

Gods:
Dionysus/Iakkhos
Hades
Helios
Hermes
Janus
Lucifer (Light Bearer)
Poseidon
Zagreus/Sabazius
Zeus

Goddesses:
Artemis
Baubo
Bendis
Bona Dea
Brimo
Circe
Demeter
Despoina
Diana
Enodia
Ereshkigal
Geneetyllis
Heqet
Isis
Kattahha/Hatkatta
Kotys
Kourotrophos
Kratais
Kybele

Medea
Melinoe
Mene
Nemesis
Persephone
Physis
Potna Theron
Rhea
Selene
Shekinah

Spirits:
Aeacus/Aiakos (Keeper of the Keys to Hades)
Angels: Wrynecks, Teletarchai, and Synocheis
Cerberus (Hell Hound)
Chthonic Spirits
Erinyes (The Strong Ones, The Angry Ones, Night Born Sisters, The Kindly Ones, Alecto-Never Ending, Megaera-Envious Anger, Tisiphone-Face of Retaliation)
Eumenides
Harpies
Incubi
Keres (Death Spirits)
Lamia
Lampades (Greek nymphs of the Underworld — Hekate's attendants and lamp bearers)
Maenads
Mora Spirits
Moerae (Fates)
Nymphs
Sirens
Strix (bird of ill omen)
Strixay
Succubi

Wind Demons
Witches of Thessaly

Often Called on Together:
Selene/Artimis/Hekate
Hekate/Diana-Luna/Proserpina
Hekate/Demeter/Persephone

Lady of Beasts

Animals, both mundane and mythical, associated with Hekate:

Bat
Bull
Cat
Cow
Crow
Dog
Dove
Dragon
Frog
Goat
Griffin
Hell Hound
Horse
Lion
Owl
Raven
Serpent
Sphinx
Toad
Unicorn
Vulture

Colors Associated with Hekate

Red
Amber
Black
Bronze
Copper
Purple
Saffron
Silver
White

Earth:
Green/Brown

Sea:
Blue-Green/Aqua

Sky:
Blue
Gold/Yellow (Sun)
Silver (Moon/Stars)

Mystical:
Red: Blood/Life
Black: Night/Mysteries
White: Bone/Death

Natural Items Associated with Hekate

Stones/Gems:
Amber
Amethyst
Bloodstone

Blue Goldstone
Emerald
Garnet
Hematite
Jet
Moon-Stone
Onyx
Ruby
Smoky Quartz
Tiger's Eye

Metals:
Bronze
Copper
Gold
Iron
Silver

Trees:
Alder
Ash
Birch
Blackthorn
Cypress
Dogwood
Ebony
Oak
Willow
Yew

Herbs:
Bay Laurel
Frankincense
Jasmine

Juniper Berries

Lavender

Mint

Mugwort

Mullein

Myrrh

Myrtle

Patchouli

Rue

Saffron

Sweet Vetivert

Baneful Herbs:

(Note: Do not use! Poisonous! Raven Grimassi wrote two books, *Old World Witchcraft* and *Grimoire of the Thorn-Blooded Witch,* that offer sigils to use when working with some of these herbs)

Belladonna

Datura

Helebore

Hemlock

Henbane

Mandrake

Opium/Poppy

Pennyroyal

Wolfsbane/Alconite

Wormwood

Altars and Offerings

As both an Earthly and Heavenly Goddess, altars and shrines for Hekate can be of varying types. A Chthonic (of the Earth) altar sits low to the ground; this type of altar is used for Underworld and Death deities. An Ouranian (of the Heavens) altar sits higher up; this type of altar is the most commonly used and is set up for deities of the Sky and Heavens. Another shrine that can be set up in Hekate's name is the Hekataion. This altar sits outside the front door of your home so Hekate can protect all who reside within.

A Deiphon or Hekate's Supper is an offering put out at a Crossroads on the night of the New Moon. Kykeon is a sacred drink thought to be made from barley, pennyroyal (poison), and water. This would have brought on a hallucinogenic trance. The Red Meal is used by Traditional and Hedge Witches, it consists of red wine and dark bread. A version of this offering can be found in Robin Artisson's *The Witching Way of the Hollow Hill*.

Offerings of drink, food, art, and sacred objects can be placed on Hekate's altar and later disposed of by burying or burning. What is offered to the Gods should never be consumed or used. These are gifts to the Holy Ones and should be considered taboo to eat unless sharing a Sacred Meal with the Gods and Spirits.

Offerings for Hekate:
Absinthe
Apples
Art
Barley
Blood
Crossroads Dirt
Eggs
Fish
Garlic
Graveyard Dirt
Honey
Incense
Mead
Milk
Mushrooms
Olive Oil
Onions

Poetry
Pomegranate
Prayers
Sacred Herbs
Sacred Objects
Scented Oils
Sesame
Song
Water
Wine: Red or White

Sacred Symbols and Objects

This is a small list of sacred symbols and objects of Hekate. She is often shown holding a few of these in Her iconography.

Athames/Daggers
Candles
Cauldron
Cemeteries
Crossroads
Gates
Hekate's Wheel
Keys
Masks
Sepulcher
Skulls/Bones
Snakes
Spear
Torches

Festivals and Dates

A few festivals and sacred dates are associated with Hekate. She, of course, can be honored at any time and I have found Her to be a very approachable Goddess who adores Her devotees.

Full and Dark Moons
Dawn and Twilight (liminal times)
Last day of every month
Deiphon: Every Dark or New Moon
Noumenia: Every New Moon (crescent)
Her Sacred Fires: Full Moon of May
January 8: Midwife Day
January 31: Feast Day of Hekate
August 13: Harvest Blessing
October 31: Samhain/Shadowfest/All Hallows Eve
November 16: Hecatesia/Hekate's Night
November 30: Day of Hekate at the Crossroads

Realms/Magic/Divination

Hekate, the Witches' Goddess, rules over many realms and is Mistress of Magic and Divination.

Realms:
Dreaming World
Elphame
Elysian Fields
Erebos
Faery
Hades
Netherworld
Otherworld
Shadow-Lands
Tartarus
The Fortunate Isle/Isle of the Blessed
Underworld

Magic and Divination:
Amulets and Charms
Blood Magic

Defixones (binding curses)

Goeteia (sorcery)

Necromancy

Nekuia (divination from the dead)

Nympholepsy (possession/seizure by Nymphs for oracle use)

Oracles

Oneiromancy (dreams/dream divination)

Pharmakeia (herbal/poison magic)

Rhizotomoi (root magic)

Tarot

Theurgia (divine/God working)

Voces Magicae (magical words)

Chapter 8

The Cunning Way

Draped by a Sandalwood and Jasmine scented mist, the Spirits of the Shadow-Lands join me in the mystical and magical dance of the Cunning Craft. Incantations are whispered, charms of making spoken in a long-forgotten tongue, and arcane symbols are drawn out with grand array. Hekate, Daemoness of Sorcery, can be felt on the boundaries of the Seen and Unseen Realms. She awaits for the moment to emerge, casting Her Sorceress Luminosity upon the Witches of the Shadow-Lands. We call Her: 'Hekate-Hekate-Hekate! Queen of Witches, Mother of Bones—come to us—your Children of the Night and Sorcery! Hekate-Hekate-Hekate!' The spell is cast, the Currents of Enchantment ride the Winds of Night, and magic fills the air...

The Cunning Craft, Sorcery, the Craft of the Wise—all these and more are terms for the spheres of enchantment and magic. Hekate, as the Queen of Witches and Daemoness of Sorcery, is the quintessential Goddess of the Cunning Way. Circe and Medea, Her eternal priestesses, called upon Hekate in times of great need, asking for Her aid in spell-craft and bewitchment. Hekate is the Holy of Holies in Witchcraft; She is great and terrible in Her making of charms and enchantments. As Queen of the Shadow-Lands, Hekate is Mother of Spirits and Ghosts, controlling the forces of the Craft who aid us.

The magic of Hekate is an Earth-based magic. The gifts of Nature are used, introducing us to the Wild-Craft that is our inheritance. We learn to live and breathe in the enchantment that surrounds us; the Earth becomes sacred and the Worlds Unseen call to us. We are enticed by the allure of connectedness; the Spirits of the Shadow-Lands become our kith and kin. The elements of Nature aid us in our Craft—Earth and Water, Fire and Air, the Fae-like Spirit that connects the Worlds, Seen and Unseen.

Till Dust Do Us Part

Enchanted Dirt has a wide variety of uses in Witchcraft and the Cunning Way. They can be added into herbal blends, charm bags, witch bottles, and the conjuring of Spirits. The magical requirement will determine the type of dirt needed. Collecting Enchanted Dirt is easy, all that is needed is a cloth bag and a tool (spoon/spade) to dig it up. A glass container or pottery with a lid can be used to store the dirt.

Graveyard Dirt

Collected at the foot or head of a grave, this dirt can be used in Necromantic and Ancestor work. When using in conjure magick, the dirt can be collected from the grave of certain types of people depending on the needed use. Always leave offerings and ask permission from the Spirit of the Graveyard and the grave you are collecting the dirt from. Pennies, dimes and rum/whiskey are traditional offerings. Remember to make 'friends' with the Dead, visiting their resting place at least once a month. Placing flowers on the graves of those Spirits you have become close to is a lovely way to thank them for their help.

Crossroads Dirt

Collected at a crossroads, this dirt can be used in the conjuring of Hekate or any other crossroads Spirit. Adding a pinch to charm bags, herbal blends, or witch bottles will add extra energy to the working. I like to add this dirt to any spell or blend pertaining to Hekate.

Deep Forest Dirt

Collected in a forest, deep enough in to get away from civilization, this dirt can be used to connect with the Spirits of

Faery. I also use this in any grounding spells and those that associate to Nature.

Shadow-Lands Dirt
Collected in any dark and desolate place on the fringes of society, this dirt connects you and any magical workings to the Spirits of the Shadow-Lands.

Dirt/Sand from Specific Places
Whether collected from a beach, mountain or desert, these can be used to connect with the energies you wish to utilize in spells and enchantments. Collecting dirt and sand from a place sacred to you can be handy as well (although check if this is allowed before taking soil, sand or stones from any important heritage sites). Dirt from a bank, court house, police station, or any other ordinary place can be collected for future magical workings.

Drowning in the Waters of Creation

Collecting waters for charms and enchantments can be as simple as setting a container out during a thunderstorm, snowstorm, or a specific Moon phase. They can be stored in glass jars or wine bottles and sprinkled on magical workings or added to your bath or cleaning water.

Moon Waters
There are a number of uses for these waters and they can be collected at the different phases of the Moon or during an eclipse. Fill a jar with the water of your choice and set it out during the chosen Moon phase. Bring it inside and place it on your altar before dawn.

Full Moon: Use for blessings, protection, and positive energy added to spells. Use to connect with the 'light' Fae.
Dark Moon: Use for curses, Necromancy, divination, and any

dark magical workings. Use to connect with the 'dark' Fae.
Lunar Eclipse Water: Use for added power and psychic workings.

Sun Water

This is a very positive water used for healing, fertility, money,
and luck and success spells. Add it to cleaning waters and washes
for a happy home filled with luck and positive vibes. This water
is best collected under the noon-day sun when the sky is clear.

Storm Water

This water is best collected during the fiercest of Spring and
Summer storms by placing a vessel outside to capture the rain.
Use it for curses, hexes and the calling of storm and wind Spirits.
Storm Water is also a very protective water. Call on Hekate, Lady
of Storms, to bless the water once it is collected.

Snow Queen Water

One of my favorite of enchanted waters, Snow Queen Water is
collected during a snow storm and the water allowed to melt on
your altar. Used it to connect with the Spirits of Winter and for
cooling or 'cooling off' in any spells. I use this water during
Summer to bring some relief from the heat and humidity.

Holy Hekate Water

Collected on any of Her holy days under the night sky, this water is
used to bless magical paraphernalia and any iconography of Hekate.
It can also be added to baths and washes to gain Her blessings.

Shadow-Lands Water

Charged on a foggy day or at dusk or dawn, Shadow-Lands
Water helps to journey to the Unseen realms of Shade and
Shadow. This can also be used for Ancestor and Necromantic
work. Call on Hekate, the Dread Queen, to bless this enchanted
water.

Queen of Sorcery Water
Charged on the night of Shadow-Fest/Samhain, this water is used for conjuring and contacting the Mighty Dead. I add a drop of Queen of Sorcery Water to many spells and charms. This is an all-purpose Witchcraft water that has numerous uses.

Crossroads Water
This is charged at a crossroads with a pinch of Crossroads Dirt added to it. Use it to connect to Crossroads Spirits and Hekate, Queen of the Crossroads.

The Fruits of Earth Bear Witness

There are endless varieties of herbal/magical blends that can be made. I love to experiment with the different kinds of herbs and powders, creating the perfect blend for charms and enchantments. The possibilities of the uses for these blends are numerous and the making of them can be a form of magic, connecting us with Nature and the cunning ways of Witchcraft. These enchanted blends can be used in charm bags, added to incense, sprinkled atop candles, added to magical oils, mixed into baths and washes, and given as offerings to the Spirits of Witchcraft.

Spirits of Elphame Blend
Used for connection to the Faery Realm, divination, second sight, prophetic dreams, and any lunar workings.

Ingredients:
Mugwort
Jasmine
Sandalwood
Pinch of Deep Forest Dirt
Drop of Moon Water

Brimo Blend
Used for protection, cursing, binding, and vengeance.

Ingredients:
Red Peppers
Black Peppers
Vervain
Pinch of Red Brick Dust
Drop of Storm Water

Shadow-Lands Blend
Used for Spirit Flight, trance, and shape-shifting.

Ingredients:
Fennel
Sage
Peppermint
Cinquefoil
Pinch of Shadow-Lands Dirt

Queen of Dragons Blend
Used for protection, defense, defeating evil spirits and bad influences, and to protect against Sorcery.

Ingredients:
Dragon's Blood
Clove
Hyssop
Nutmeg
Star Anise

Dame Venus Blend
Used for love, lust, beauty, seduction. To contact and connect with the Queen of Elphame, Dame Venus, Sirens, Nymphs,

Leannan Sidhe, and Fetch-mate.

Ingredients:
Rose
Rosemary
Vervain
Apple Seed
Coriander

Bone Mother Blend
Used for Necromancy, contacting the dead, Fate-Weaving, and contacting Old Fate and the King of the Underworld.

Ingredients:
Cypress
Juniper
Sandalwood
Patchouli
Drop of Pomegranate Juice

Hekate Soteria Blend
Used for health and healing spells, exorcism, and the banishing of spirits and gloom. Used to bring happiness, harmony, and light into the home.

Ingredients:
Cinnamon
Chamomile
Saffron
Allspice
Frankincense

Dark Muse Blend
Used for creativity, connecting with the Muse, Green Fairy

contact, Leannan Sidhe, La Fee Verte, and poetic inspiration.

Ingredients:
The three Holy Herbs of Absinthe:
Wormwood
Anise Seed (not Star Anise)
Fennel

Herbs that can be added for extra strength:
Star Anise
Hyssop
Calamus
Angelica
Coriander

Add three drops of Absinthe to finished blend.

Queen of Sorcery Blend
Used for Sorcery, Cunning Craft, conjuring of Spirits, contacting the Witch Mother and Father, Shadow-Fest/Samhain, and Spirit Flight.

Ingredients:
Myrrh
Rue
Mugwort
Bay Leaf
Drop of Queen of Sorcery Water

Spirit of the Crossroads Blend
Used to connect with Hekate and other Spirits of the Crossroads, protection, and petitioning Hekate for help with Spirit contact.

Ingredients:

Yarrow

Anise

Cumin

Frankincense

Pinch of Crossroads Dirt

The Dead Will Rise

Necromancy, the act of raising the dead for divinatory workings, is a long lost arte. Hekate, Queen of the Dead, was said to aid those who wished to use this unsavory act of Sorcery to reanimate the dead. In today's world, Necromancy covers all works of magic concerning our Beloved Dead. It is used to contact the dead in hopes of gaining their help in the making of charms and enchantments. The Spirits of the Dead dwell in the Shadow-Lands and the Lands Below. They are kin to Faery and are known to haunt the same grounds. The arte of graveyard and cemetery magic is a form of Necromantic Sorcery.

Hekate's Death Demons and Lampades can be called upon to aid in Ancestor and Necromantic workings. Making contact and befriending these Nymphs of the Shadow-Lands can be very rewarding for they are Hekate's Children just as we are. They are our kith and kin and, like family in the waking world, the Lampades can be fiercely loyal.

A separate altar for the Beloved Dead should be prepared and tended lovingly. I always light a candle and set a fresh glass of water on the altar every day. Prayers can be said and petitions made with offerings appropriate to the Spirit being contacted. How you decide to decorate the altar for the Beloved Dead is up to you and the Spirits you are devoted to. The collecting of Memento Mori can be a rewarding pastime and hobby as it connects us to our Beloved Dead.

In the Land of Milk and Honey

The true essence of Faery lies within the heart of the Witch — our blood quickens with promise of power and deep connection with those Unseen. To see through the looking glass of time and realize that all that is thought to be real is but an illusion; a mere reflection of what we wish to be — who we can be — and who we are meant to be. Fated by She who controls the gossamer webs of Life and Death, our lives can be filled with enchantment if we just open ourselves to the possibilities.

What we make of this world and how we interact with it determines our happiness and our unique perspective on the Seen and Unseen worlds. The Threads of Fate are intertwined with our co-walkers — our Faery-selves. This world, so full of beauty and enchantment, is a sister to the Realms of Faery. Earth, our sacred home, is part of Faery — it is Faery and we are Her children. When we begin to treat Her with the compassion and respect She deserves, we begin to see the World for what She truly is — *Life Enchanted*.

Kalliste Hekate, the Fair Queen of Elphame, can be found guarding the Gates between this world and the next. She is the Opener of the Ways, the one who gives us true sight so we may see the Worlds for what they are — the Elysian Fields of old. The Great Sorrow of the today is the forgetfulness we have encountered in this life. We must awaken to the World of Faery, stirring the ancient memories of our Beloved Dead. The search for Faery can be found in the Whispering Hills of the past, present, and future.

Faery has not returned to us, rather, we have returned to Faery. We, as Witches and Pagans, have begun to feel and see our connection to the Enchanted World we live in. There is much wisdom to be gained from Hekate and our Faery Lovers and Selves if we just open ourselves up to the concept of our *otherness*. To do that is as simple as befriending the Spirits of Faery and the Shadow-Lands. Invite your Faery Lover into your life, welcome him/her with open arms and heart, allowing the primal nature of ecstasy to consume you. Call on the Leannan Sidhe, the Eternal Nymphs of sexual desire and inspiration to aid you in the finding of your Faery Lover. When you have been re-united with your other half, your Faery Lover, you will know what it is to feel complete. Your Faery Lover will be with you in Life and Death, they are a part of you, and they always have been and always will be.

On the Wings of Spirit We Fly

Hedge-Crossing, Hedge-Riding, Wind-Riding, and Myrk-Walking; these are just some of the terms for Spirit Flight. It is a journey you take in Spirit form or in the Dream World in which we meet at the Witches Sabbath or join with our Fetch Beast in the making of magic. While Hedge-Riding, we are able to journey to realms we cannot get to in the waking world. In Spirit form we can ride the Current of Enchantment to worlds Unseen, the kingdom of Faery and the Shadow-Lands.

As we attend the great feasts at the Witches' Sabbath provided by Hekate, Queen of Witches, we ready ourselves for the Night Battles. We side with the Benandante—Good Walkers—Seelie Court, or with the Malandante—Bad Walkers—Un-Seelie Court, in a battle for the good of the worlds, Seen and Unseen. Of course, who are we to decide what is good for the Worlds; what may seem virtuous in Faery may in reality be immoral in the waking world. Things are not as they seem in the Realms of Shadow and Enchantment; beware of who the true monsters are.

There are many ways in which we can travel to the Spirit Realms, finding what works for you can take many attempts of trial and error. Swaying, drumming, hissing, dancing, and deep meditation are just a few ways of gaining access to Spirit Flight. The creation of Flying Ointments can be dangerous if toxic herbs are used in their making. There are ways to make the ointment without the dangers of poisonous herbs, finding the right concoction for you is the trick. Again, it's all about trial and error; that, of course, is what's so rewarding about Witchcraft—the magic and enchantment that fills our lives.

Once we find our method of flight, we whisper upon the Winds of Change the destination we wish to visit. Here, we can fly on the Witches' Broom, change shape into bird or animal form, or take on the visage of our Faery-Self. When we arrive, the time for magic and mayhem begins. We join others in the Dance of Enchantment and prepare for the Battles of Night. We watch as the Wild Hunt swarms the worlds Seen and Unseen and we join in the Feast of the Wicked.

To return to the Realm of the Living, a simple wish upon the Winds of Change and visualizing our corporal bodies will help us to awaken and come back to ourselves. The eating of solid foods and engaging with our family or pets will help to ground and center after a night of Hedge-Crossing. Though you may find it hard to travel in the beginning, after much practice you will find that with ease you can slip into the trance-like state needed for the Spirit-Flight. Believing in yourself is the key to any form of magic and enchantment.

The Arte of the Damned

Witchcraft is terrifyingly beautiful and insanely ecstatic. It is who we are, our blood is aroused and our eyes opened by the Dance of Life and Death. To be a Witch is to awaken to our true selves, the mysteries of the Worlds are ours to discover and embrace. The finding of our Familiar/Fetch Beast is akin to finding a long-lost loved one. They are part of us and are the key that unlocks the Gates of Faery, the Shadow-Lands, and the Witches' World of Enchantment.

Our Familiar/Fetch Beast may be bodied or pure spirit. They may be animal, part animal, or humanoid. Familiars/Fetch Beasts have mastered the arte of shape-shifting, they have learned to ride the currents of Witchcraft, flying off to aid us in the making of charms and enchantments. They can take the form of dragons, griffins, gargoyles, and other mythological beasts. At times nothing more than a cloud of smoke, our Familiar/Fetch Beast is always with us, comforting in their very presence in our lives. To form a loving relationship with our Familiar/Fetch Beast will ensure a lifetime of enchanted companionship.

You cannot summon the Familiar/Fetch Beast, they will make themselves known to you when the time is right. They are with you from the beginning and will be with you in Death. When you feel the rustling of your Familiar/Fetch Beast it will be accompanied by a deep sensation of love and longing. If it is fear you feel, then either you are not ready or this is not your Familiar/Fetch Beast. Cleansing and the setting of wards will aid in non-friendly Spirits harassing or trying to contact you.

The cauldron and the stang/staff are the two tools I use most often in my craft (besides my mind and spirit). The stang aids me in access to the World Tree and the cauldron aids in the access of Hekate's Cave. Both connect me with the Realms of Faery and Shadow, allowing me to ride the Currents of Enchantment. The stang/staff can be decorated with horns, antlers, and feathers and the cauldron can be a cast iron cooking pot or any other vessel you feel drawn to. There are many other tools that I use in the Craft—a wand, knife, herbs, and enchanted waters all aid me in their own unique way.

The life of a Witch is one filled with enchantment, the worlds Seen and Unseen carry with them the knowledge of the Beloved Dead. The Blood of the Witch has awakened as we join in the Ecstatic Dance of Faery and Shadow. Magic can be found everywhere, the key to finding it lies within the Heart of the Witch and Faery. As our lives converge on the World of Enchantment, we become one with Nature and Hekate. Like Circe and Medea, we are Her Children of the Night.

Conclusion

As I close my eyes and fall into the Deep Trance of the Dreamworld,
I find myself at the entrance of Hekate's Cave. The scent of burning
herbs lingers in the moist, ocean air. Softly glowing within are
candles inscribed with occult seals and sigils; enchantment
emanates all around me. She is standing there, Queen of the
Witches, stirring Her Cauldron of Transformation. I look deep into
the contents of this sacred vessel and find my destiny within. I am
transformed now, a Daughter of Hekate and the Sacred Feminine.
The Witches' Blood that courses through my veins has awakened, I
am now One with Hekate and the Spirits of the Worlds—Seen and
Unseen...

She is all around us, our Witch Mother Hekate. She is the beauty
of a sunset and the terror of a storm. She is of the Moon, the
Stars, the Sun and the Earth. She is of the Sea and the Abyss, the
primal Catalyst of Creation. I have found Her in the Deep
recesses of my mind, and have wandered far within my dreams
in search of Hekate and the Holiness that She is.

Whether we see Hekate as the Witches' Goddess, Queen of
Heaven, Dread Goddess, or World Soul does not matter. She is
all of these and more; new facets of Her are being discovered by
those who wish to journey to meet this Great and Terrible Queen
of Mysteries and Magic. She may show us one side of Herself or
many, depending on the nature of Her call. The paths we choose
to take on this sometimes perilous expedition can lead to great
wonders. The arcane truths of the Realms of Eternity can be
found both within ourselves and in the finding of our Sisters and
Brothers who join us in this Dance of Life and Death. To awaken
the Blood of the Ancients is to awaken to our true selves, our
most magical and enchanted selves that we are destined to be.

Hekate, Queen of Witches, welcomes Her Children into the

Mysterious world of the Shadow-Lands, encouraging us to spread our wings and fly into the enchanted Beyond. We must continue to bring Her into the Waking World, the mundane world we live our daily lives in. The more we honor and devote time to this most Gracious Queen can help others to awaken to the Mysteries of the Enchanted Realms, the Ancient Ones, and Faery.

Hekate, my Queen, I give thanks to You as I continue on this Journey of Life and Death. As my Dreams become Reality and Reality become my Dreams, I weave Enchantment and Deep Peace into the Worlds as Your Devotee and Daughter. Hekate, Holy Mother of All, I am Yours and through Your Grace I Live and Breathe... May I find comfort within Your embrace...

Recommended Reading

Classical Volumes
Greek Magical Papyri (PGM)
Medea by Euripides
Metamorphosis by Ovid
The Chaldean Oracles
The Homeric Hymns
The Orphic Hymns
Theogony by Hesiod

Modern Texts on Hekate
Bearing Torches: A Devotional Anthology for Hekate by Bibliotheca Alexandrina
Evoking Hecate by Anousen Leonte
Hecatean Magick by B. Morlan
Hekate Soteria by Sarah Johnston
Hekate: Her Sacred Fires by Sorita D'Este
Hekate: Keys to the Crossroads by Sorita D' Este
Hekate: Liminal Rites by Sorita D'Este & David Rankine
The Dance of the Mystai by Tinnekke Bebout
The Temple of Hekate by Tara Sanchez

Other Books of Interest
A Deed Without A Name by Lee Morgan
Apocalyptic Witchcraft by Peter Grey
Between the Living and the Dead by Eva Pocs
Blood in the Bayou by Docteur Sureaux
Cunning Folk and Familiar Spirits by Emma Wilby
Encyclopedia of 5000 Spells by Judika Illes
Encyclopedia of Spirits by Judika Illes
Grimoire of the Thorn-Blooded Witch by Raven Grimassi
Masks of the Muse by Veronica Cummer

Old World Witchcraft by Raven Grimassi
Sorgitzak-Old Forest Craft by Veronica Cummer
Sorgitzak II Dancing the Blood by Veronica Cummer
The Faery Teachings by Orion Foxwood
The Flame and the Cauldron by Orion Foxwood
The Living World of Faery by R.J. Stewart
The Mighty Dead by Christopher Penczak
The Tree of Enchantment by Orion Foxwood
The Underworld Initiation by R.J. Stewart
The Witching Way of the Hollow Hill by Robin Artisson
To Fly By Night by Veronica Cummer
Vampyre Magick by Father Sebastiaan
Vampyre Sanguinomicon by Father Sebastiaan

Tarot and Oracle Decks
Les Vampires Oracle by Lucy Cavendish & Jasmine Becket-Griffith
The Tarot of Delphi by J.D. Hildegard Hinkel
The John Waterhouse Oracle Deck by Tarot by Seven, LLC
The Faeries' Oracle by Brian Froud & Jessica Macbeth

MOON
BOOKS

Moon Books invites you to begin or deepen your encounter with Paganism, in all its rich, creative, flourishing forms.